HOT and BOTHERED

Also by Jane Isenberg
in Large Print:

Midlife Can Be Murder
Mood Swings to Murder
The M Word
Death in a Hot Flash
Out of Hormone's Way

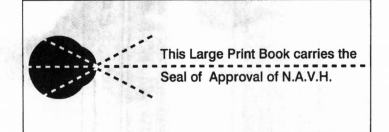

HOT and BOTHERED

A Bel Barrett Mystery

JANE ISENBERG

WHEELER
PUBLISHING

Published in 2004 by arrangement with Avon Books, an imprint of HarperCollins Publishers, Inc.

Wheeler Large Print Softcover.

The text of this Large Print edition is unabridged.
Other aspects of the book may vary from the original edition.

Set in 16 pt. Plantin by Ramona Watson.

Printed in the United States on permanent paper.

Library of Congress Cataloging-in-Publication Data

Isenberg, Jane.
    Hot and bothered : a Bel Barrett mystery / Jane Isenberg.
       p. cm.
      ISBN 1-58724-780-1 (lg. print : sc : alk. paper)
      1. Barrett, Bel (Fictitious character) — Fiction.
2. Stripteasers — Crimes against — Fiction.   3. Women college teachers — Fiction.   4. Middle aged women — Fiction.   5. Hoboken (N.J.) — Fiction.   6. Scholarships — Fiction.   7. Large type books.   I. Title.
PS3609.S46H67 2004
    813′.6—dc22   2004053573

To the members of my writing group,
Susan Babinski, Pat Juell, and
Rebecca Mlynarczyk,
with love and appreciation for the wisdom,
support, affection and desserts you have
shared with me during the past twelve years

As the Founder/CEO of NAVH, the only national health agency solely devoted to those who, although not totally blind, have an eye disease which could lead to serious visual impairment, I am pleased to recognize Thorndike Press* as one of the leading publishers in the large print field.

Founded in 1954 in San Francisco to prepare large print textbooks for partially seeing children, NAVH became the pioneer and standard setting agency in the preparation of large type.

Today, those publishers who meet our standards carry the prestigious "Seal of Approval" indicating high quality large print. We are delighted that Thorndike Press is one of the publishers whose titles meet these standards. We are also pleased to recognize the significant contribution Thorndike Press is making in this important and growing field.

Lorraine H. Marchi, L.H.D.
Founder/CEO
NAVH

* Thorndike Press encompasses the following imprints: Thorndike, Wheeler, Walker and Large Print Press.

ACKNOWLEDGMENTS

Much of this book takes place in a Hoboken neighborhood, and for helping me to keep that neighborhood alive in my imagination, I thank Augusta Pryzgoda, President of the First Ward Block Association. Thanks also to Gene Turonis, otherwise known as Gene D. Singing Plumber, for his music. And thanks to Steve Nuding for sharing his renovating expertise with me for many years. Susan and Hubert Babinski, Elaine Foster, Marge and Bill Graham, Dr. Annette Hollander and Myron Kaplan, Pat and Tom Juell, Peggy McGeary and Ruth and David Tait have all earned my gratitude for housing me when I traveled to New Jersey to do research or readings.

For their understanding, support, and guidance during a stressful year I thank my editor, Sarah Durand, and my agent, Laura Blake Peterson. New friends here in Massachusetts have also nurtured me as I wrote, for which I am very, very grateful. When my husband, Phil Tompkins, and I moved last Fall, Daniel Isenberg and Shilyh Warren packed and stored over sixty boxes, and Shirley and Paul Tompkins came and helped us unpack them. Rachel and Jordan Stoner flew across the country to offer hands-on assistance when Phil was convalescing, and Brian Stoner provides invaluable guidance as we contemplate our next move. Phil continues to be a demanding first reader and willing webmaster (wwwJaneIsenberg.com), as well as an example of great courage, strength, and wit.

CHAPTER 1

To: Bbarrett@circle.com
From: Rbarrett@uwash.edu
Re: block party rsvp
Date: 10/01/01 10:20:16

Mom,

Thanks for the invitation to the block party. It's cool that it's happening regardless of the attack on September 11. I'm really proud you all decided not to let the terrorists cause you to break with neighborhood tradition. The block party is sacred. We kids used to wait all year for that one day when everybody moved all the cars off our street and closed it to traffic. Luci Aquino and I roller-skated for hours trying not to crash into all the little kids zooming around on their big wheels. It was totally happening.

I remember one year when some lame oldies band started playing "Earth Angel" and you and Daddy tried to dance. Ohmigod, that was so mortifying I wanted to move. And remember the time Mark ate too many hot dogs and threw up all over our stoop? And the year you had to take him to the ER because he broke his wrist skateboarding? I wish we had parties like that out here. No, what I really wish is that I could come back to Hoboken for the block party and bring Abbie J. But I have work and classes, so . . . you and Sol should party for us. Say hi to all the neighbors for me especially Luci if she comes back.

Love,
Rebecca

E-mail from my daughter never failed to dislodge whatever people and events had been preoccupying my mind before I read it. My students at River Edge Community College in Jersey City, New Jersey, faded into a sepia-stained blur in the background of my consciousness. They were displaced by an image of Rebecca's blond hair and green eyes shining as brightly as those of her daughter, Abbie J. My only grandchild appeared as a color-splashed collage of purple jelly stains on a yellow shirt, grass green overalls, and her red fireman's hat. Abbie J would have loved the face painting at the block party! As a little girl, Rebecca had always asked for whiskers and cat eyes. Her brother Mark had insisted on smearing camouflage colors over his freckles himself. As I reread Rebecca's message, even concern about my beloved partner Sol became muted, displaced by the memory of his grin after he scored the winning point in the volley ball game at a long-ago block party.

But before I got too lost in my memories of block parties past, the doorbell chimed. I heard it during a momentary lull in the screech of the electric sander in the kitchen. This sound, somewhere between the screams of mating cats and an ambulance siren, had been the background music for our daily life since the kitchen renovation began during the past summer. Picking my way carefully through the array of power tools and stacked lumber that now filled most of the downstairs of our row house, I opened the door to Professor Eunice Goodson — colleague, student, neighbor, and secret stripper.

As the noise assaulted her through the open door, Eunice, a stern-looking, stocky, and bespectacled young woman in her late twenties with a persistent tan, stuck her fingers in her ears in the time-honored manner of seasoned New York subway riders hearing a train enter the station. Eunice was one of the few people I know who could look dignified with her fingers in her ears. Eyes bright behind her metal-framed granny glasses, she smiled and said, "Hi, Bel. Am I early? Remember, I promised I'd stop for you on my way to the meeting?" Signaling for her to wait, I went back inside, grabbed my purse

11

and the folder next to it, stuck my head into the kitchen area, and waved good-bye to our carpenter. In the few seconds of silence that accompanied his mock salute, I said, "Ed, be an angel and let Virginia Woolf out of the bedroom when you leave." As soon as Ed arrived each morning, I incarcerated my favorite feline in the bedroom, where she spent the day ensconced in a basket of unread *New Yorkers*.

My duty done, I joined Eunice on the stoop, pulling the front door shut behind me. "Sorry about the din. We're renovating our kitchen," I explained. "Thanks for rescuing me. Another two minutes in there and I'd be stone deaf." I shook my head as if doing so would exorcise lingering echoes of the shrill noise. "So, Eunice, how's the apartment working out?" I asked as we began to walk.

"Bel, I can't thank you enough for that lead. I had hoped to room with my sister, but . . ." Without finishing her sentence, Eunice said, "The place is perfect. As soon as I get settled, I'd like you and your husband to come over." I didn't bother interrupting Eunice to explain that although Sol was the love of my life, he and I had not chosen to formalize our long-standing living arrangement. "I am just so grateful," she continued. Eunice's gratitude was understandable. Affordable apartments in Hoboken were still rarer than a bag of M & Ms at a

Weight Watchers' meeting. But a couple of weeks earlier my old friend and neighbor Felice Aquino had mentioned that in the wake of the terrorist attack she had a vacancy. The occupant of her basement studio apartment was moving to south Jersey where his company, whose former address had been in Tower 1, now planned to relocate permanently. I suggested that Eunice call Felice. Then I called Felice myself and put in a good word for Eunice.

"Felice is pretty pleased too," I said. "She's so glad you're quiet and don't have a lot of rowdy company or play loud music. Her last tenant tried to re-create that special frat house ambiance by hosting raucous parties till all hours. She says she never hears you."

"Well, I'm not there that much," Eunice said, glancing at me conspiratorially. "Club girls don't exactly keep bankers' hours." Her grin softened the contours of her square jaw. Eunice's direct reference to her "day" job did not take me by surprise. A new member of the adjunct faculty at River Edge Community College, where I had been teaching for decades before my first gray hair or hot flash, Eunice taught anatomy to prenursing and funeral services education students. She was also enrolled in a faculty development seminar I was leading to help new faculty with pedagogy and classroom management.

I had asked the group to write an introductory essay. In hers, Eunice confided that she had long aspired to teach anatomy. "I think the human body is one of nature's miracles, and I want to help others to appreciate it" was how she put it without a trace of irony. Her large upstate New York farm family had no money to spare for college and less understanding of why their brainy daughter might want to leave home to go to one. Eunice had gone anyway, putting herself through the university and grad school by dancing in strip clubs. "I didn't want to graduate with one of those big loans you read about," she had written.

But even though she had earned her master's degree and finally had students of her own, Eunice couldn't afford to stop dancing because, as a part timer, she did not earn nearly enough money to support herself. Or, as she put it, "I don't intend to lower my standard of living now that I'm teaching." Even though my inner sixties-style feminist recoiled at what I perceived as Eunice's willingness to objectify herself, I admired her determination and resourcefulness. Besides, she had the makings of a damn good teacher. I hadn't mentioned Eunice's other line of work to Felice. "I don't come out to most people," Eunice had explained, "but I could tell you'd understand. After all, you kept a perfectly straight face when Nelson Vandergast told the whole seminar that when he isn't teaching he leads tours of New Jersey sites featured on *The Sopranos*."

I smiled at the recollection of Nelson's revelation. But dancing in Manhattan strip joints was a far cry from accompanying tourists on a quick trip to the real Bada Bing Club. I wondered about the hours club girls kept and if it was safe for Eunice to be taking the train back to Hoboken alone in the early morning. But Eunice was my colleague, not my kid, so before I responded, I repressed my knee-jerk Jewish mother's admonition and replied, "Felice says you offered to feed her cat while she's away. That earns a lot of points around here." As we dodged a cyclist while crossing the street, I continued. "Ten years ago we all had children who would tend to plants, pets, and mail if a neighbor went away, but now our kids have grown up and moved out, and it's hard to find somebody who will take on a finicky and ferocious critter like Felice's Amos." I sighed the sigh of a cat owner who has had to entrust her own pampered pet to the haphazard care of a harried adult neighbor instead of to the devoted ministrations of an animal-loving ten-year-old. My own Virginia Woolf had survived the lackadaisical attentions of several adult caregivers only by virtue of her feline ability to suspend herself regally over the toilet bowl and sip water.

"Of course. That's what I would have done

15

back home," said Eunice. Did she sound a little wistful? I wasn't sure. "Sounds like you all have been here forever. That's what I miss most, being part of a community." She shifted her focus abruptly. "But, Bel, are you really sure I should be serving on this committee? I'm so new here. Won't people think it's presumptuous of me?" We had almost reached the Shannon Lounge, where members of the Park Avenue Neighborhood Association's Block Party Committee held its meetings. I had wanted the PANA Scholarship Committee to meet at my house, but when the upheaval of renovation made that impossible, I asked the others to meet me in the back room of the Shannon. The familiar beer-and-smoke-soaked confines of this as yet ungentrified bar were an unlikely place for a scholarship committee meeting, but this was an unlikely committee.

"Everybody will welcome a new face," I said. At least I hoped they would. Some of my neighbors resented the hordes of upwardly mobile young people who had invaded their mile-square town, changing it from a bastion of blue-collar workers and immigrants to an upscale postcollegiate bedroom community. The newcomers didn't give a damn about Frank Sinatra, let alone where he was born. I hoped the native Hobokenites among my neighbors wouldn't think Eunice was a typical yuppie. Stifling my concern, I added,

16

"So many of the tenants on the block don't get involved. And remember, you're a professor. That'll go a long way with these folks." It went a long way with me. I hoped that the neighbors would embrace Eunice so that the following year she would take over my responsibilities as head of the PANA Scholarship Committee.

"Who are the other members? Felice and you are the only neighbors I've met," said Eunice, still sounding a bit anxious.

"There are only three besides us," I said holding down a finger as I summoned each name from the recesses of my unreliable memory. "Tony Delgado is a widower who teaches gym at a parochial school, Delphine Arledge is a young feminist artist, and Joey Petrone, otherwise known as Joey P, is a retired railroad worker. They'll be glad to have you." I gave Eunice a reassuring pat as I nodded at the bartender, who was on the phone in the otherwise empty saloon, and headed for the back room. The morning-after silence of the bar was a welcome contrast to the cacophony of the ongoing renovation at home.

"Where does PANA get the money to give out a scholarship?" Eunice asked as we settled ourselves around a scarred table to wait for the others.

"We owe it to our first treasurer. What *is* his name?" Silently I cursed the midlife memory loss that made certain names as inaccessible as a winning lottery ticket. "It'll come to me. But whoever the hell he was, he made a few good investments of dues and block party proceeds, and now we use the interest on those CDs along with some pretty decent earmarked donations," I said aloud.

A rare moment of modesty prevented me from mentioning that the PANA scholarship had been my brainchild. Years ago I had persuaded the group to give a full one-semester grant each year to a neighborhood kid who either attended or planned to attend RECC. I had agreed to chair the committee for the first year, but no one had taken over my duties, and as the years went on I just kept convening the same committee, reviewing the applicants, and awarding the grants. Lately this had not been very onerous since, over time, the number of kids in our neighborhood had decreased, and for each of the two preceding years there had been only one applicant. The annual decision had been easy to make.

I didn't know it then, but that year was going to be different.

CHAPTER 2

To: Bbarrett@circle.com
From: Mbarrett@hotmail.com
Re: Block party blues
Date: 10/01/01 12:15:25

Yo Ma Bel,

So it's time for that slammin', jammin', happenin' rite of autumn, the annual PANA block party, where the kids all over-dose on sugar and soda and the geezers sit around on lawn chairs sipping beer and watching them! Except for you and Dad. Remember that time you two tried to dance to some lame oldies band? I was so embarrassed I nearly fell off my skate-board. I think that was the night I broke my wrist, remember? Hell, I'd have done anything to get you two to stop dancing. I remember you had to take me to the ER and there was a guy ahead of me who had just gotten shot.

Jason and I used to skate after the little kids on their big wheels and terrorize them. That was awesome. And remember one year Rebecca and Luci Aquino hung out on Felice's stoop all afternoon in those tight shorts trying to get her nerdy yuppy tenants to notice them? Well, even though Aveda and I can't make it down there to party with you this year, I'm glad the terrorists didn't screw up that event for everybody else. That would have sucked. The rockin' PANA Block Party lives! Gotta go back to work.

Love,
Mark

Delphine Arledge arrived at the Shannon just after Eunice and I had settled at a table. I had to smile. The young painter's magenta-tinted cropped curls and Spandex T-shirt emblazoned with Old Glory and ending inches above her bejeweled navel seemed more appropriate to an exotic dancer than did Eunice's muted gray shell, tailored black slacks, and tied-back brown shoulder-length hair. Sitting next to Delphine, Eunice looked demure, even severe. *Eunice is dressed like a feminist,* I thought, *and Delphine, a bona-fide second-generation feminist, looks like a stripper.* Still smiling, I introduced the two women.

Just then Tony Delgado and Joey P entered the back room of the Shannon. As usual the two old cronies were arguing. "No, we gotta have the block party. It's like our tradition. We can't let them take that away too. If we didn't have it . . ." Tony paused in his con-

20

versation with Joey P, as if even contemplating the travesty of a blockpartyless season had rendered him speechless. Delphine and I exchanged glances, aware that the familiar debate about whether or not to have canceled the party was being rehashed even though the decision to go ahead with it had been made, flyers printed and posted, and the food and band arrangements reconfirmed.

"If we didn't have it, you'd miss out on your chance to boss everybody around for a day, that's what," said Delphine. She spoke with easy affection and moved her enormous color-splashed tote bag off the chair next to her to make room for Tony.

"Look, Delphine brought her whole apartment," said Tony, nodding in the direction of the huge vermilion, gold, and green sack, which now took up a fair amount of space on the floor between them.

The retired gym teacher, whose personal fashion statement still involved a whistle and sneakers, and the thirty-something artist, who favored Doc Martens and body piercing, traced their unlikely friendship back to the death of Tony's beloved wife, Angie, two years earlier. A few weeks after she died, and the postfuneral deluge of casseroles and floral tributes ended, Tony emerged, unshaven and blinking in the sunlight, to begin trudging up and down the block in search of a few groceries and the local paper. His newly solitary trek took him by Delphine's stoop, where she often sat reading the late afternoon paper and chatting with passersby. She was shocked by the change in her neighbor's appearance and showed up at his door with a bottle of Chianti and a care package of frozen chicken Marbella that her mother had brought her. When she asked him if she could paint a portrait of Angie from a photo for a show she was having in the spring, Tony decided it didn't matter if Delphine wore loud clothes and had an extra hole in her nose, she was good people. And anyone Tony thought was good people was okay by Joey P.

That's why Joey P wasted no time in responding. "I see. I see. You gotta pay admission for that thing if you bring it to the block party? Does it count as a dependent on your tax return? Could you maybe, you know, deduct it?" Joey P's voice, sanded to a whispery rasp by too many cigarettes, lent an eerie edge to almost anything he said. Delphine wrinkled her studded nose at him.

"Hi, Bel, good to see you," said Tony, grinning in my direction and eyeing Eunice with frank curiosity.

"Yeah, Bel, I run inta Sol once in a while on the block, but I ain't seen you in a long time. Where ya been keepin' yourself?" Joey P took a seat on the other side of Delphine. Before I had a chance to reply, he nodded to Eunice and said, "You live in Felice's building, right? I seen you movin' your stuff in. You the new tenant?"

"Yes. I'm Eunice Goodson." Eunice extended her hand. "And you are?"

Eunice and I both had eleven o'clock classes, so I figured it was time for me to try to make this ragtag collection of neighborhood eccentrics function like the committee we were supposed to be or we'd just sit around chatting all morning. "Joey Petrone and Tony Delgado, this is Eunice Goodson, our new neighbor and a colleague of mine at River Edge Community College. Eunice teaches anatomy. I've invited her to join our committee now that Angie's gone." A shadow darkened Tony's face at the mention of his late wife's name. I saw Delphine reach out and squeeze his shoulder. "Eunice, these two guys are founding members of PANA. They've lived here forever. Delphine's literally a new kid on the block. She's only been here five years." There was a flurry of nods and smiles. Eunice looked relieved.

I was wishing I'd thought to bring a cup of tea because everybody but Eunice and I was sipping liquid caffeine from Styrofoam cups. Feeling deprived, I sighed and took out copies of the scholarship applications and distributed them. "Thanks to all of you for serving on this committee and for agreeing to meet this morning. Now that the block party is definitely on, we're in a bit of a rush. I

23

know I don't have to remind you that everything we say here is confidential. This year we have two applications. That hasn't happened in a long time. But it poses a problem for us." I paused, acknowledging the puzzled looks my comment had evoked as everybody glanced at the names on the applications and then back at me.

"I don't see no problem, Bel," hissed Joey P, putting the papers down in front of him. I could tell he had made up his mind without even reading them through. Briefly I wondered if I should have removed the names, but that wouldn't have helped.

"Me neither," said Tony. "One of these two deserves it. The other doesn't."

"It looks pretty clear-cut to me too," said Delphine.

Eunice had no opinion but rather waited for me to explain. I took another sheaf of papers from my folder and distributed them around the table.

"What's this here? The PANA bylaws," Joey P said, answering his own question. "What do we got to do with them, Bel?"

"Okay, here's the deal as I see it. The problem is that one of the two applicants for this year, Yronellis Illysario, won this scholarship last year," I said, leafing through the bylaws for the section I wanted to read.

"Yes, she did," said Delphine. "Yronellis is a very deserving young *woman*." She looked around the table as if defying anyone to contradict her. "And Dennis Denoya?" She made a dismissive gesture with her hand. "No way," she said crossing her arms over the American flag on her chest. I wasn't really surprised since Delphine had confided to me that Dennis had hit on her several times at last year's block party and had been calling her ever since, refusing to be discouraged by her rebuffs.

"Yeah. And look," Tony was pointing at one of the pieces of paper in front of him. "Yronellis has a 3.8 average. That girl made good use of that scholarship we gave her. And another thing, how long has her family been living here? That kid's lived here longer than you have, Bel." The tendency of my neighbors to first pose and then answer their own questions usually amused me. That morning, it was beginning to get on my nerves. "She's lived here her whole life," Tony added. It was clear to Tony that the fact that Yronellis had been born and raised in Hoboken more than qualified her for another scholarship. Tony had leaned over to make his points, and when he finished speaking he sat back in his chair. Now it was his turn to look around to see how we had reacted to his diatribe.

I decided to hold my tongue, and Joey P spoke. We all leaned closer to hear him. "No way we give it to the Illysario kid again. She had her turn. Let's give somebody else a chance. Dennis got a raw deal when that hotshot computer company he was workin' for went belly up. Listen, ya gotta give the guy credit. He's tryin' to make something of hisself, right, Bel? That's why he's goin' to cookin' school." As if to highlight his point, Joey P crushed his now empty coffee cup and pitched it at the wastebasket in the corner of the room. It went in.

Before I could answer, Eunice spoke. "Bel, what do the bylaws say about awarding the scholarship to the same person more than once?" All heads turned in her direction. I could have kissed her.

"Funny you should mention it," I said. "Just take a look on page three, third paragraph. See, right under PANA Scholarships." I began to read. " 'Any resident of the block who is currently attending RECC or who has preregistered for the spring semester is eligible to apply for the annual PANA scholarship.' Applicants are required to provide two letters of reference and a complete transcript." I put the paper down and said, "That's all it says about the scholarships. This never came up before."

"Well, maybe it shouldn't come up now," said Delphine, sounding put out. "After all, the way I see it is if it's not mentioned in the bylaws, we can pretty much do what we want."

"You just don't want a man to get the scholarship," said Tony.

"I certainly don't want that dot-com loser to get it, you're totally right," said Delphine, gesturing in the direction of what I took to be Dennis's application on the table in front of her. "Besides, a scholarship should cover a whole year, not just a semester. Yronellis deserves our support for an entire academic year. Then we can review the bylaws."

"The kid is right," said Tony, smiling at Delphine. "And I hate to say it, but you, my friend, are wrong." He looked at Joey P. I braced myself for one of those long arguments the two old pals enjoyed inflicting on the rest of us. Like my mother and her housemate, both widows, these two lonely old men argued out of habit. "Besides, think how proud Ilona will be. And she should be." Ilona was Yronellis's mother. There was no doubt that she had been lobbying on behalf of her daughter. "She told me that kid studies all the time."

Joey P said, "Good for her. Now let's give somebody else a break."

"Actually, I think Delphine has a point." Eunice smoothed back a stray hair as she spoke. "We really should review and clarify the bylaws. It would be better to do that first than to establish an unfortunate precedent by giving the scholarship to the same person two years in a row. We should poll the mem-

27

bership and see how they feel about the whole thing and rewrite the bylaws to reflect what the majority wants."

"I agree with Eunice and Delphine," I said. It had been shrewd of Eunice to pick up on a portion of Delphine's comment and use it to support her own view. I figured I might as well jump on the same bandwagon. "After all, this committee is not supposed to make rules. We just carry them out," I continued. "If you really don't think Dennis is a deserving candidate, we might consider not awarding the grant at all this year."

"Who says Dennis ain't a deserving candidate?" It was Joey P taking his turn now at brandishing Dennis's application. "Look, he's got a letter here from one of his profs at college sayin' what an inventive and, how do you say it, enterprenial mind he's got."

"That's the problem. Don't you get it?" said Delphine, exasperation making her voice shrill. "Dennis already has a college degree. He had his chance. He blew it. If we're not giving it to Yronellis, Bel's right, we shouldn't give it to anybody."

"But what's wrong with giving somebody a second chance?" asked Eunice. "That's what community college is for. I don't know this Dennis or the young woman either, but he has a very respectable transcript and glowing references. And the letter he wrote explaining why he wants the scholarship is very moving." I saw Eunice glance at her watch as she brushed back that straying strand of hair. "I move that we offer the scholarship to . . ." she quickly eyeballed the paper she held in her hand, "Dennis Denoya." I was as impressed by my young colleague's command of parliamentary procedure and her cool head as I was by her concern that she get to her class on time. I guess if you could dance nearly naked in front of total strangers, you could make a simple motion in a small meeting.

"Anybody second that?" I asked, picking up the ball Eunice had thrown and running with it.

"Yeah. I do," said Joey P.

"Any discussion?" I didn't want to be accused of railroading a vote through without giving everybody a chance to be heard.

"I've said my piece," said Delphine.

"Me too," said Tony.

"I'd like to amend Eunice's motion to include Delphine's point about asking the bylaws committee to review the bylaws pertaining to the scholarship by next year," I said.

"Hear, hear!" said Delphine. "I second Bel's addition to the motion."

"Anybody else have anything to add now?" When no one did, I said, "How many in favor?" Eunice and Joey P raised their hands. After a second or two, Delphine poked hers

29

into the air, perhaps realizing that it was capricious not to vote for a motion you had seconded. "Opposed?" Tony's hand went up. I was relieved that I didn't have to break the tie. "Well three in favor, one opposed, so this year's PANA Scholarship goes to Dennis Denoya. I'll speak to the Executive Committee about initiating a review of the bylaws for next year. Good work everybody. Thanks for coming."

Not surprisingly, Tony was fuming. "I've known that girl since she was in diapers," he was saying to Joey P as, our job done, we gathered up our things and headed for the door.

"So have I," said Joey P. "So I know Yronellis Illysario was a brat in diapers and she's a bigger brat now. She had her turn. Whatcha got against givin' Denoya a chance ta, ya know, get back on his feet?"

"But it's not right that someone who just moved here should . . ." I didn't hear the rest, but I hoped that Joey P could talk some sense into his old buddy before Tony, in spite of the confidential nature of our committee's work, found a way to badmouth Eunice by telling anyone who would listen that she was an intrusive newcomer trying to take over.

CHAPTER 3

**River Edge Community College
Faculty Development Seminar
— Handout 3 —
Excerpts from participants' essays on
"My Biggest Problem As a Teacher Is":**

Nelson Vandergast: Some students come in to my Intro to Management class late no matter how many times I threaten to lower their grade in the course.

Eunice Goodson: When I give a lecture I've spent hours preparing, some students write grocery lists, doze, or doodle instead of taking notes. I'm not used to an inattentive audience. What should I do?

Dinesh Shah: Yesterday before the commencement of my Basic Math II class I overheard a student imitating my particular accent. Some of them say they don't understand me. I say too bad. Globalization is here.

Eleanor Marshall: In Western Civ I, we have to cover the Stone Age through the

Renaissance in one semester, so I assign two or three chapters a week and my students say that's too much reading.

Barbara Sternfeld: Many of my students don't know much grammar or punctuation. A few of them can barely speak English let alone write it. It takes me hours to . . .

On Tuesday night I was still typing the handout when I heard the phone ring. I remembered to click on SAVE and weight the pile of papers I was culling the excerpts from with my mug of tea so they wouldn't fly all over the place. Then I ran to where I thought I'd put the handset after I'd finished the last call. It wasn't there. For a frantic moment I felt nostalgic for the days when the receiver was attached to the phone by a cord. Even though you couldn't take the phone into the shower with you then, at least you always knew where the damn thing was. I located it coated with plaster dust on that catch-all table near the front door where the folder of student papers I was working with had turned up earlier that morning. I grabbed the phone just before the fourth ring.

"Hi, *chiquita,* thanks for inviting us to the block party. Raoul and I have a date to go shopping for a new dishwasher this weekend, but we'll try to stop by when we're done." It was Illuminada Guttierez, my friend and colleague. Like Eunice, Illuminada taught part time at RECC. And like Eunice, Illuminada had a challenging day job. She had parlayed her one-woman crusade to find deadbeat dads and get them to cough up child support into a high-profile private-investigation firm. They did everything from background checks to undercover work unmasking pilferers, embezzlers, and good old-fashioned adulterers. Just as I was now mentoring Eunice, I had once mentored Illuminada. In fact, it was Illuminada who had inspired me to write the grant that resulted in the Faculty Development Seminar. "Bel, you're a hidden treasure. You should try to share your experience with as many people as possible," was how she had put it. That was just after we had worked together with Betty Ramsey to figure out who killed RECC's first woman president. We three had been friends ever since.

"Oh good. Sol will be pleased. I've asked Betty and Vic and, of course, my mother and Sofia. Why don't you bring your mother too? If the weather holds, it should be relaxing. We can just sit around and talk and eat and then, if you want, you and Raoul can show us all up on the dance floor." I wanted to host friends at the block party because the dust and debris from the renovation made our home a highly undesirable guest destination.

"I don't know about my mother and I don't know if we'll feel like dancing, but the rest sounds good," said Illuminada. Milagros Santos, Illuminada's mother, lived upstairs from Raoul and Illuminada and occasionally joined us at parties. "My mother's been sticking close to home lately, but I'll ask her. She hasn't been driving me too crazy. And speaking of crazy, how's the renovation going, or shouldn't I ask? Is your miracle worker, Ed, making any progress? Tell me, do you think I should ask him for an estimate on enclosing the porch on my mother's apartment?"

"I would. But you know how we feel about Ed." I looked around at the devastation that had once been our kitchen and closed my eyes, trying to imagine how it would look when it was finished. Buoyed by this vision, I went on. "Ed's repaired or rebuilt everything in our house at least twice. And he's done the same in Felice's house and a lot of others on this block. He just finished renovating Felice's new shop too. Remember I told you her bridal shop relocated to the Avenue?"

"No, but I'll take your word for it," said Illuminada.

Encouraged, I continued my sales pitch. "Ed does really fine carpentry and he sticks to his estimate."

"He's pricey, though, right?" Illuminada asked.

"He's not cheap, but he's experienced and reliable." I paused, aware that I had sung Ed's praises to Illuminada before.

"Okay. I'll ask him to give us an estimate. What harm can it do to ask?" Illuminada sighed. Even contemplating the ordeal known as home improvement was tiring.

"None, but you should be aware that he probably can't do the work right away. He has a long list of prospective jobs and he'll put you on the end of it," I explained, recalling how many months we'd had to wait for Ed to be available to begin work on our kitchen. "But I'll introduce him to you at the block party. That way he'll know who you are when you call him," I said, welcoming the chance to connect Ed with a prospective client.

"Okay, *chiquita*. But tell me, did Betty say she and Vic would come?" Illuminada sounded worried.

I understood and shared her concern. We had all been badly shaken by the terrorist attack on September 11. But like Sol, our friend Betty Ramsey, executive assistant to RECC's president, had been more upset than most. Her only son Randy had recently started working on the fiftieth floor of Tower 1 at the World Trade Center. When Betty saw the plane hit and then the next plane hit and then the buildings burn and fall, she had been certain that Randy was trapped in the inferno. For hours she had stared at the TV in the student cafeteria, picturing her son being incinerated in a stairwell or an elevator or jumping from the fiftieth floor. She was too numb to pray, to cry, to move.

In fact, Randy had started his workday with a breakfast meeting at a midtown bank, so he was on the subway en route downtown to the office when the first plane hit. Not quite absorbing what was going on, he had tried to reenter the building but had been denied access by a firefighter. Also too numb to cry, to leave, or to phone, he stood on West Street, his back to the river, watching the free-falling paper, people, and furniture, When he finally collected himself and joined the hordes of terrified folks fleeing the site, he tried to reach Betty, but his phone didn't work. By the time he finally got her, she had aged twenty years.

"Betty hasn't gotten back to me. That's so not Betty," I said. I pictured Illuminada nodding on her end of the phone line. The Elizabeth Ramsey we knew and loved was efficient to a fault. "I'll call her and ask her again," I added. "I'll call Vic too. Maybe he can persuade her to show up for a while." Betty and Vic, the world's most unlikely couple, had met while we were investigating the death of Vinny Vallone, Vic's brother and partner in Vallone and Sons Funeral Home. Vinny had been teaching part time at RECC.

36

To everybody's astonishment, Vic, an easy-going and affable Italian American, and Betty, a workaholic African American with a penchant for control, had fallen in love. Even more remarkably, they had stayed in love. If anybody could persuade Betty to join us, Vic could.

"Good idea. I'll e-mail her," said Illuminada. "She'll come round. After all, Randy is already back at work in a new location."

"You know, I think that's at least part of what's bothering Betty. Randy's been working down in south Jersey for now, but his company is renovating a building in Connecticut. He'll probably get an apartment up that way as soon as the company relocates," I said. "Betty likes having Randy living in Jersey City, where she can keep tabs on him." Illuminada and I both sighed audibly, recalling our mutual friend's need to control.

"I know. Well, let's see if we can get her to that party, even if it's just for a little while. Talk to you later." Illuminada's good-bye left me holding the filthy phone with one hand and brushing plaster dust out of my hair with the other. I checked my messages and found one from Eunice. "My schedule at the club is changing, so I might have to miss the first few minutes of the seminar this week. I hope not, but I wanted to let you know just in case."

I didn't get to finish typing my handout for

the faculty development seminar until the morning the group was to meet. I noted gratefully that Ed had retaped the plastic dropcloth over my computer and printer. This would help a little, but even though I'd moved the computer to the bedroom the night before Ed began to work, I feared that the poor machine would never be the same. There was no time to brood over that though. After I printed the handout, I took it to RECC to Xerox and distribute. The seminar was going reasonably well, and I thought it was time to address the issues raised by the comments I had collected from the participating teachers.

When I got to the room where we met, I was surprised to find Eunice already seated, her notebook open. I was glad that her new schedule was not going to interfere with her attendance. I began class on the dot of two with a half-hour lecture on the nontraditional student. I used no visual aids. Nelson and Dinesh were five and ten minutes late respectively. While I was talking, I walked around the back of the circle we were in and jotted down the names of the three individuals who were not taking notes. To the consternation of the group, halfway through the lecture I began speaking faster and with a heavy Yiddish accent. It was pure Yentl meets Our Miss Brooks. I followed the lecture with an essay test on the week's reading, which had consisted of two ten-page articles, one on nontraditional students and the other on differing learning styles.

Since this was a stunning departure from the progressive pedagogy I'd been modeling for the first few classes, everyone was shocked. When I collected the papers, there was a storm of protest and not a little apologizing. "I couldn't get here earlier. My class ran over. I had to explain the last problem three times," whined Dinesh.

"I was at a committee meeting and it lasted forever," said Nelson. "I couldn't just walk out while the dean was talking. That would have been rude." It did not seem to have occurred to him that some profs might have considered his late arrival at our seminar rude too. "Can I get the first part of the notes from somebody?"

"Does that test count? I didn't think we were getting graded in this seminar," Eleanor said. "If it's going to count, may I do a retake? I don't write well under pressure."

Eunice had taken notes and wanted to discuss the content of my lecture. I looked forward to that discussion. But before that, I distributed my handout and asked them to use it as a jumping-off point for dialogue with their writing partners and preparation for their next writing assignment, an essay to be entitled, "Why I Am a Nontraditional Student." As the group divided into pairs, I said, "We are not really so different from our students, are we? In fact, we're nontraditional students ourselves." There were smiles and a few people nodded, recognizing the truth of my statement.

The partners arranged their chairs a few feet away from other pairs and began to talk quietly to each other. I wanted to teach them how to use twosomes as an alternative to the traditional teacher-centered class discussion. To model how to facilitate these conversations, I circulated, eavesdropping on each twosome and occasionally offering a comment or posing or answering a question. Eunice, her glasses in one hand, a wadded Kleenex in the other, was speaking earnestly to Nelson. She looked to be on the verge of tears. "I worked so hard dancing in clubs to put myself through school, just so I could teach. But teaching's not like I thought it would be. I don't understand some of these kids. Most of them are going to be nurses or undertakers and they really have to know how the body works, but they can't be bothered taking notes or . . ."

"You were, like, a stripper?" Nelson asked, his voice lowered. "For real?"

A frown that momentarily creased Eunice's forehead and then disappeared was the only sign that she was annoyed at what her partner had chosen to extract from her heartfelt words. "Yes. It pays better than waiting tables or shelving stock or working a cash register at Wal-Mart. And the hours are more flexible," she explained patiently. "Lots of students do it."

"But why would you degrade yourself that way?" Nelson was leaning forward now, his voice suddenly urgent.

I was about to intervene when Eunice, apparently no stranger to this sort of reaction to her chosen night job, said with the same aplomb she'd displayed at the PANA Scholarship Committee meeting, "Look, I appreciate your opinion, but do you mind if we get back on topic here? My point is I'm used to having people pay attention to what I do. I'd appreciate some suggestions on how to get my students to tune in to my lectures. How do you get your students to listen to you?"

Confident that Nelson would now respond appropriately by sharing some of his own teaching strategies, I moved on. Every fifteen minutes, I asked one member of each couple to join another partner so that by the time I reassembled the large group, everyone had spoken with at least three different people. Nelson and Eunice left the room together, talking animatedly.

CHAPTER 4

Save the date!
Saturday, October 20, 2001
Park Avenue Neighborhood Association's
FALL BLOCK PARTY
noon till midnight

Park Avenue between 2nd and 3rd Sts.
Catch up with old neighbors and
meet new ones!
Refreshments all day, volleyball,
kids' games and face painting, and
announcement of winner of 2001's PANA
Scholarship!

Dancing at night to the sound of
PANA's own Gene "D" Singing Plumber!

Members $5 Nonmembers $10

Raindate 10/21/01

This year a portion of the proceeds will go
to a fund for families of victims of 9/11.

The block party fell on one of those perfect Indian summer days that we had been

perversely gifted with during that cataclysmic fall. The bright sunshine and unseasonable warmth brought out the neighborhood neatniks all ready to sweep early in the morning. I was not among them. Since the terrorist attack on the World Trade Center, I'd resumed attending synagogue on Sabbath mornings. Sabbath worship, a habit I'd only begun cultivating when preparing for my adult bat mitzvah, had been a casualty of the Saturday mornings I'd spent as faculty advisor to the RECC Urban Kayaking Club the previous spring. I shuddered, recalling the grisly murders that had become indistinguishable from that experience and blighted it in my memory.

The sight of Sol brandishing a broom delivered me back to the present. Unfortunately, since September 11 the present had been blighted as well, and Sol was living testimony to that fact. His stocky frame appeared less substantial and his eyes, normally mischievous, were now more often wary. I was worried about him. Like Betty's son, Sol had been enroute to the WTC on the morning of September 11 and had witnessed the buildings' destruction. But whereas Betty's son had been on the subway, Sol had been aboard the ferry. Badly shaken by what he had seen, he feared more terrorist attacks.

But that morning he had joined our neighbors to prepare for the block party. He was sweeping fallen leaves and scraps of litter from our gate, the vernacular term for the concrete area in front of a row house. As soon as the street was completely cleared of cars, Sol and the other gate sweepers would turn their attention to what was to be our communal patio for the next fifteen hours.

Sol and I were sharing a good-morning hug when Joey P came rushing over to us looking flustered. His simple words would have sounded ordinary a year earlier. That year they had the ominous ring of prophecy. "Jeez. I was tryin' ta move my car but they got cops all over the Avenue." For reasons lost in local lore, Hoboken's main drag, Washington Street, is always referred to as "the Avenue." "Traffic's backed up for blocks."

Delphine, Felice, and Tony, all engaged in sweeping their gates, put down their brooms and gathered around the tall gray-haired man. Sol, his brow suddenly rutted with worry lines, asked, "What's going on?" I resolved to try not to focus on Sol's anxiety. I wanted to believe that, given time, this retired economics prof would recover the self-possession and wry sense of humor that had attracted me to him when we first met. That had been years before, when we were both active in the Citizens Committee to Preserve the Waterfront, a group determined to stave off those developers hoping to play high-stakes Monopoly along Hoboken's strip of riverbank.

"A cop told me," Joey P wheezed, "that there was an unmarked package delivered to Swift Savings this morning. They don't know what's in it. The cops are waiting for the bomb dogs and then if it's not a bomb, they'll take it to examine for traces of . . ."

"Anthrax . . ." everybody intoned in unison, a Greek chorus articulating one of our newest and worst fears.

A hefty woman with tufts of red-orange hair and the social style of an antebellum plantation overseer showed up just then. It was Ilona Illysario, and she spoke with her usual authority, an authority derived largely from being married to the PANA president and mother of last year's PANA scholarship winner. "It's not a bomb and they've already taken it away for testing. So let's get this place cleaned up. Remember, the kids gotta make chalk drawings on that concrete. Move it guys!" She grabbed her broom and headed for the street to begin sweeping the gutters where earlier the cars had obscured the week's accumulation of litter and leaves. Sol looked only slightly relieved, but by the time I left, he had finished sweeping our gate, bagged the debris, and joined several others in the now nearly carless street.

By the time I returned three hours later, inspired by Rabbi Ornstein-Klein's sermon and by the comforting familiarity of timeless songs and chants, our block had completed its annual metamorphosis. Felice's three granddaughters were drawing on the pavement with colored chalk, while some other youngsters, perhaps Ilona's grandkids, had lined up beside Delphine and were waiting patiently for the smocked and grinning artist to paint their faces. Tony's grandson was the solitary skateboarder, and a crowd of yuppies had emerged to use the volleyball net for a spirited game accompanied by good-natured cheers and hollers. I recognized Dennis Denoya in the front row, where he was providing useful if noisy assists.

A row of grills lined the street in front of Tony's house, and there Sol, Joey P, Ilona, Ed, and Tony were talking animatedly while nursing charcoal fires not yet quite hot enough to begin grilling the hundreds of hot dogs, burgers, and sausages from coolers behind them. At a discreet distance, Eunice was helping Tanya and Ignacia set up the vegetarian table, an attraction that had grown over the years from a token tray of crudités to a colorful feast of appealing alternatives representing the many cuisines of our neighbors. There were still crudités, but now they shared space with curries, samosas, humus, tabouli, eggplant parmigiana, assorted salads, potato and cabbage pirogies, ratatouille, and even a veggie tagine. At the end of the block opposite the volleyball court, neighbors and their guests had begun to set up lawn chairs in familial clusters. Nearer the middle the committee had arranged a few large round tables.

I noted that Sol had staked out one of these for us, draping several chairs with his signature blue Citizen's Committee to Preserve the Waterfront windbreaker and covering a few others with my green RECC sweatshirt. Felice had commandeered a table nearby. I figured she was closing the shop for the day. I looked around for Ma and Sofia, but they hadn't arrived yet. Seeing that Ed was manning a grill, I was tempted to retreat into the house to take advantage of the rare moments of peace and quiet there. But rather than face the grime and mess, I ambled down the block to the Illysarios' shaded gate, where it had become traditional to place the trash cans full of ice, soda, and beer.

Grabbing an iced tea, I nodded to Yronellis, who was sitting on her stoop. With her was a sad-eyed, black-haired girlfriend and two little boys who looked like Yronellis's sister's kids. The boys were showing off their newly painted faces and the girls were manicuring each other's nails. "Hi, Bel, I mean Professor Barrett," Yronellis said. Her eyes did not quite meet mine, so I suspected that she already knew she would not be the recipient of this year's PANA Scholarship.

"Hi, Yronellis," I answered, smiling, and wondering which committee member had blabbed. I resolved that the following year I would really stress to the scholarship committee the importance of confidentiality. Keeping secrets had never been the strong suit of anybody on our block. Sooner or later, everybody found out everything about everybody else. When somebody was ill or in trouble, the word got out fast, help came, and we congratulated ourselves on our neighborly network. When somebody came home drunk, didn't come home, got arrested, or was experiencing more than the usual amount of domestic difficulty, the word traveled equally rapidly, and then we deplored our penchant for gossip.

But at that point nobody seemed to know about Eunice's other life. Not that anybody would really care, at least not the young people, I figured as I watched my colleague arranging plastic utensils in Styrofoam cups and placing the cups in an orderly row at the end of the veggie table. Like the denizens of most really cosmopolitan enclaves, our neighbors were a pretty live-and-let-live bunch. Even so, some of them would be shocked if they knew that, in a matter of hours, the bespectacled young woman unwrapping packages of plastic plates and making small talk would be peeling off her clothes while gyrating in front of an audience of leering men. Sitting there sipping my iced tea, grateful for the stellar weather and mindful of the flags that had sprung up like late-blooming blossoms in windows and on fences up and down the block, I realized that I too was shocked by Eunice's job.

"Here we are, Sybil." I winced at the sound of my full name, something that no one but my mother had used in at least forty years. Ma's announcement had effectively interrupted my moment of self-discovery. "Marie left us off at the corner," said Ma, sounding just a little winded. I offered a silent thank-you to Sofia's daughter for saving me the trouble of getting the car from whatever place Sol had found to park it for the duration of the party. "Looks like everybody's working here but you. You got the right idea. It's good to see you sitting down for once." Automatically I stood and held a chair for Ma and then for Sofia as the two octogenarians settled in for an afternoon of chitchat and high-cholesterol fun. The fact that Sofia was a Hoboken native meant that she knew most of the lawn-chair crowd, and I knew that they would be stopping by to pay their respects en route to the food tables. A little American flag cleverly crafted of safety pins and beads decorated each woman's lapel.

I was about to ask where they had gotten the pins when Sofia said, "I see Sol's at the grill again. How's he feeling?"

49

Before I could update her on Sol's post–September 11 mental state, Ma said, "Here, Bel. These are for the dessert table. We didn't want to come empty-handed." She reached into a large bag at her feet and produced a cardboard pastry box from Georgio's tied with red-and-white string. At the sight of it, I salivated. "We got a couple dozen of the little cannolis. Why don't you take them over?"

"Sadie, don't forget," said Sofia, pulling a smaller version of the same box out of the bag so we could see it and then putting it back.

"I'm not forgetting anything," said Ma. "We got a little box specially for Sol in case the others get eaten before he gets a chance to have any." I smiled. Once Ma had finally accepted my divorce from Lenny, whom she, in total ignorance of his real nature, had prized as a prince among men, she began to appreciate Sol. Their relationship had evolved into a mutual admiration society that, quite frankly, bordered on the mushy. In fact, Sol had become a favorite with both women since he often took them shopping and to medical appointments.

"You know what he wants?" Ma began.

"Yes, and I don't want to talk about it," I snapped. "I have no intention of retiring early," I said, trying to temper my tone and repress my annoyance that Sol had even

50

mentioned this cockamamie notion to my mother. What was the man thinking? Or *was* he thinking? "And I have no intention of moving to the country either," I said, eager to put to rest any anxiety Ma might feel at the prospect of our moving. "So let's just relax and try to enjoy the afternoon. After all, you two didn't give up a day in Atlantic City to sit and talk nonsense." I wasn't kidding. Their days at the casinos kept these two inveterate gamblers going. "Look, the dogs and burgers and sausages are on the grill. Can I make you two a plate? I'm taking orders."

"Thank you, Bel, dear. I'd like some eggplant and a sausage-and-pepper hero, please," said Sofia in that effortlessly polite tone we reserve for the relatives of our friends.

"What about you, Ma? I know you want the eggplant. How about a hot dog and a little kraut?" I asked, knowing what the answer would be.

"I'm going with you, Sybil. I don't need you to wait on me. She just wants to sit here like the Queen of Sheba and gossip with her old crowd," said Ma, gesturing at Sofia. I could tell that she was a bit discomfited by how many people her housemate knew. Ma could never remember the names of all of Sofia's friends and relatives no matter how often Sofia introduced her to them.

A bit later on, Sol took a break from the

grill and joined us to sample his own cooking. I felt it was my patriotic duty to have a burger and a dog. There would be time for the veggie stuff before the band started.

No sooner had Sol sat down than Illuminada and Raoul arrived. *"Buenos días,"* said Illuminada, bending to kiss Ma, Sofia, and Sol. Raoul had stopped to exchange greetings with someone he knew at Felice's table. "Isn't this incredible weather? Any sign of Betty?" When I shook my head, Illuminada frowned and went on, "She e-mailed that she'd come, but I had the feeling she was just humoring me so I'd stop bugging her."

"Let me look at you, dear," said Ma, pointing to an empty chair next to hers, and Illuminada promptly sank into it. I hoped Ma wasn't going to go on about Illuminada's brush with breast cancer the previous year. Ma proceeded to give Illuminada the once-over, taking in the tiny crow's feet and the web of fine lines radiating from the corners of her mouth. "Just as beautiful as ever," she said. I was relieved that my sharp-eyed mother did not elaborate on the fact that since Illuminada's diagnosis and treatment she had begun to show signs of age. But Ma, a two-time cancer survivor herself, was right. With her sleek black blunt cut framing her thin face and bright eyes, my friend *was* just as beautiful as ever.

"She's even more gorgeous, this woman is," said Raoul, coming up behind his wife and bending down to embrace her. "And so are you," he said gallantly taking Ma's hand and planting a kiss on her knuckle. I swear she blushed every time he did this. He glanced toward Sofia, prepared I felt sure to expound upon her beauty as well, but she was deep in conversation with a cousin who had moved out of town and whom she didn't see very often.

"So what's the matter, I don't look so hot?" said Sol, getting up to shake hands with his friend. I was relieved to hear the ironic inflection in his question. He sounded more like himself.

"Well, *amigo,* your problem is that you are not a beautiful woman," said Raoul. "That stuff looks good. What is it, eggplant parmigiana? Nothing like buying a dish-washer to make a man hungry. Want me to get you a plate, Mina?" he asked.

"No, thanks. I'll go over in a minute. I just want to get comfortable first. Bel, can I use your bathroom?" Illuminada asked.

"Of course. Go right upstairs and use the one in the bedroom. The other one is full of spackle cans and the lights don't work. Be careful you don't trip on anything. Wait a second. I better go with you. If you do trip over something, you might sue us," I said, surprised I could joke about the mess in our house that was driving me a little crazier each day. It was as if the chaotic state of our home mirrored the chaos of the rest of the world just when I needed a refuge from that turmoil.

By the time Illuminada and I emerged from the house, PANA president Charlie Illysario had rigged up the microphone and was standing in front of it. "He's probably going to announce the winner of the PANA Scholarship now," I said. Charlie gripped the mike in one hand and held up the envelope I had given him with the name of the latest winner. A short, portly man with a shock of black hair, Charlie began his remarks by asking for a moment of silence in memory of those who had died on September 11.

When he resumed speaking, his voice was still somber and somewhat at odds with the warmth of his greeting. "So a hearty welcome to the twenty-fourth annual PANA block party. It was not an easy decision we made to go ahead with the party, but seein' everybody here on this beautiful day, I'm glad we did. We got a twenty-four-year tradition behind us and we're gettin' ready to celebrate our twenty-fifth anniversary of this event next year. But I'm gettin' ahead of myself here.

"First I wanna be sure and thank all the committee members who been workin' hard to keep this wonderful tradition of ours going, not just this year, but every year. You know who you are. A lot of work goes into gettin' the permits, arrangin' the food, hirin' the band and cleanin' up later. And speakin' of cleanin' up, most of you know the drill by now but if yer a first-timer, listen up." Charlie looked over in the direction of the volleyball players and sighed, since after the moment of silence the yuppies had resumed their game. His sigh contained all the disapproval this jovial and generally forgiving man allowed himself.

"The last dance you do is after the band stops. For that one yer partner is a big garbage bag. Just make sure that all the trash is bagged and all the tables, chairs, grills, and the volleyball net get off the street. Then you can start bringin' yer cars back," Charlie went on, still clutching the mike. "And now, it is my very great pleasure and pride to introduce the winner of last year's PANA scholarship, none other than my own daughter, Yronellis Illysario." While not thunderous, the applause was pretty loud, especially from the table where Ilona presided over a gaggle of relatives. Felice and Tony shared a nearby table, and Tony was clapping as loud as he could too.

Yronellis, in a simple white T-shirt and pencil-legged jeans, teetered to the mike on high platform shoes. "I want to thank you all for raising the money to make this scholarship possible. It was a big help to me to have it this year because I didn't have to work and I could concentrate on my grades. I'm going to major in business, and just to let you know you got your money's worth, I had a 3.8 GPA last semester," said Yronellis, walking into Charlie's arms for a hug. Then we all clapped as she teetered back to her family's table.

"And now it is my pleasure to announce the winner of this year's PANA scholarship to River Edge Community College," bellowed Charlie as, with gravitas worthy of a Nobel presenter, he opened the envelope I'd given him. He removed the sheet of paper, glanced at it, and proclaimed, "The winner is Dennis Denoya. Dennis, will you please come up here?" Charlie reached into his pocket and pulled out the envelope containing the actual check as Dennis, wearing shorts and sneakers and sweating from his exertions on the volleyball court, made his way to the mike.

"Thank you all for giving me the opportunity to change my life. As most of you know, I'm out of a career, so I'm going to River Edge Community College to study to become a chef. I appreciate your taking a chance on me. People like you who are willing to give somebody a second chance remind us what this country of ours is all about." Instead of heading back to the volleyball courts, Dennis walked over to the line of grills and took his place where Sol had stood. His short speech and this gesture of solidarity inspired considerable applause from every table but the one occupied by Yronellis, where the table-hopping Tony had just taken a seat next to Ilona. Tony whispered something to her, and she glanced over to where Eunice had been serving vegetarian food.

I looked around for Eunice, hoping she was taking as much pleasure in the way this was turning out as I was. When I finally spotted her, a small figure carrying a large black shoulder bag, she was nearly to the corner and headed in the direction of the PATH train, no doubt on her way to work.

CHAPTER 5

To: Bbarrett@circle.com
From: Egoodson@hotmail.com
Re:
Date: 10/13/01 15:45:17

Professor Barrett,

I'd like to put together a website for my classes. Could we have a session on that? I'm friendly with the woman who designed the site for the Big Apple Peel, the club where I work, and she'll help me with the technology, but I'd like some ideas about what to include besides the syllabus and course calendar. Maybe study questions on each chapter in the text and some topics for consideration or is that overload?

Thanks,
Eunice

As I watched Eunice walk away, I recalled her recent e-mail message. It remained in my in-box with several others. They would all have to wait. It was, after all, the weekend. Anyway, Eunice wouldn't have time to log on for an answer now that she had left for work, poor girl. She was missing the best part of the block party. The band was playing and even the Sinatraphiles on lawn chairs couldn't resist tapping their feet to "A Six-pack & You" and "I Love You (and I Love Somebody Else Too)," staples of D. Plumbers' repertoire. Gene D. Plumber was a Hoboken plumber who also sang, played guitar, and wrote songs. I remember thinking how it was too bad that Eunice couldn't have stuck around long enough to hear the band's warm and wild music. It would have been a fitting finale to her initiation into our neighborhood.

But Eunice couldn't miss a Saturday night of dancing at her "day" job, even to hear a plumber making music at his night job. As I contemplated the irony of that fact, it struck me that not many of us at the block party were dancing. The mood that evening was decidedly low key. Perhaps we felt more like catching up with our neighbors because the terrorist attack just across the river had renewed our appreciation for each other.

Or maybe we weren't dancing because there were so few kids around. Luci Aquino had not made it back. In fact, Yronellis and her girlfriend, still camped on their stoop, were the only neighborhood offspring in sight, and they looked bored. Unwilling to take the few steps across the divide separating the newcomers from the tightly knit ranks of the born and raised, the two girls made no effort to connect with the yuppies camped on a stoop across the street. Of course, the yuppies stayed put too. I smiled as I recalled Rebecca and Luci's brash block-party tactics. The thought of Rebecca made me wonder what the point of dancing was if you couldn't mortify your kids. And I smiled again.

"What the hell are you looking so happy about? Is it because you're moving? I never would have pictured you and Sol leaving Hoboken. Tell me it's not true, Bel." Felice fired these questions at me as she pulled up a chair at our table and sat down. Her sharp tone told me she was serious.

My mouth opened before I could stop it, but no words came out. Felice and I had raised Luci and Rebecca together. We had bonded as only first-time moms can while pushing strollers and eating leftover squashed PB and J sandwiches. As the girls grew up we'd seen less of each other, but we still shared a certain closeness that was almost familial. That's probably why Felice's barrage of bizarre questions came as such a shock that I was unable to reply.

In even less time than it takes for a skyscraper to collapse, my shock turned to anger. Of course I was angry at the terrorists who had changed our world forever, but they weren't around for me to blame. Poor Sol was. And he just didn't get it. First of all he was telling people we were moving when I'd never agreed to such a thing. Nor would I. I loved Hoboken. One of the things I loved about Sol was that he too loved Hoboken. Besides, Ma was here, and she depended on us to maintain the delicate ecosystem she needed to continue to live "independently." My work was here. Our friends and neighbors were here, and we needed each other more than ever now. For better or worse, Hoboken was home.

I turned to glare at Sol, who had just come back from dropping Ma and Sofia off. He looked out of sorts himself. I was too angry to trust myself to speak to him at all, let alone to thank him for taking Ma and Sofia home. Because of the ban on cars, Sol hadn't been able to park in our usual spot in a vest-pocket lot across the street. He had probably been driving around for ages trying to find a place to leave the car until the block party was over and he could drive it in. He wouldn't be the first person whose urge to move out of Hoboken was validated by the shortage of parking spaces. He looked tired and put out.

As if to confirm my impression, he said, "Jesus, it's impossible to park in this town. I've been going round in circles for almost forty-five minutes. I couldn't even get it into a garage. I tried, believe me, I tried." His usually rich bass voice sounded nasal and kvetchy. I was still so annoyed with him that I felt little sympathy. "Anybody else want a beer?" he asked, looking from Felice to me. When neither of us took him up on his offer, he headed for the Illysario's stoop. I saw him retelling his sad and familiar tale to Tony, Joey P, and Ed, who were seated there, tapping their feet in unison to the music.

"Who told you we're moving?" I asked Felice, relieved that I had recovered enough to respond to her inquiry.

"Tony and Joey P were talking about it. I think Sol mentioned it while they were grilling burgers this afternoon. So, it's true, isn't it, Bel?" The longer I let her go on, the more upset my old friend became. "Oh, Bel, we've been here for each other for over twenty years. Who will I talk to if you leave?" She was working herself into a state and spit out her next two questions in an accusatory tone. "Is that why you're finally fixing up your kitchen? To jack up the sale price of your house?"

"Relax," I said, leaning over the arm of my chair to give Felice a clumsy hug. "We're not going anywhere. Sol's just letting off steam. He's got a good case of post-traumatic stress syndrome, I swear. Remember I told you how he saw the whole World Trade Center disaster from the ferry? Well he's still upset, that's all.

With time he'll recover just like the rest of us will. Put it out of your mind. It's not happening," I said, wondering how many other people Sol had shared this little bit of misinformation with. Had he confronted Ma and Sofia with it again on the drive home? I really didn't want Sol to keep upsetting Ma with his crazy ideas. Actually, I didn't want him to be having crazy ideas. That was usually my territory.

Later that evening after the band had played their final tune, a soothing rendition of "Sentimental Journey," we began the familiar ritual of cleaning up. We filled trash bags with litter that the sweepers, moving more slowly than in the morning, pushed into piles. Then we distributed these sacks in gates up and down the block so that no one family would have too many to put out for trash pickup on Monday. People took apart the grills, emptied more ice into the coolers to store the leftover meat, and reclaimed their empty pie tins and casserole dishes. With the help of Dennis Denoya, Ed dismantled the volleyball net that Felice would store in her shed until the following year. By the time the band had packed up their instruments and sound equipment, the street was clean and empty, ready for the influx of cars. One by one, people left on foot to round up their vehicles and drive them back to the block, relishing their annual chance to park within a few steps of their houses.

Sol was so tired from his unaccustomed exertions that he didn't seem to notice that I barely spoke to him as we made our way through our downstairs trying not to bump into the uprooted old appliances or boxed new ones. Plaster dust and sawdust still covered everything, including Virginia Woolf, who was sitting on our bed energetically licking her newly gray fur. I wondered how long it would be before she threw up.

"The party was pretty blah tonight, didn't you think, love?" asked Sol as he peeled off his jeans.

Briefly I wondered if we'd been to the same party. "Low key and mellow, yes. Blah, no," I answered, staring around me at the filthy warehouse our once bright and inviting bedroom had become. Both our computers and the printer had been relocated here as well as those knickknacks I wouldn't entrust even to Ed. My entire collection of china shoes filled four cartons that were stacked at the foot of the bed. And in spite of the fact that we kept the door to this connubial sanctuary closed, everything bore a telltale patina of plaster dust. "This entire place is a sty. I'm taking a shower," I announced, feeling the grime filtering into my nose, settling on my scalp, and irritating my already dry eyes.

"Good idea. Mind if I join you?" Sol asked, feigning gallantry. We often showered together, an experience that, depending on our mood and circumstances, could be either companionable or erotic. That night it was neither. We showered in silence, soaped each other's backs with the efficiency of long practice, and took turns standing under the spray while rinsing away the lather. If Sol noticed that these ablutions were hardly amiable, he gave no sign. I required no help toweling my back or applying moisturizer to my dry postmenopausal hide. By the time we made our way to bed, I was seething, but determined to save my recriminations until morning since I knew it was too late and we were too tired to begin a truly satisfying fight now. Contrary to what the relationship gurus in the women's mags advise, after fifty, it's better to go to bed livid than to have a late-night argument.

I gingerly pulled back the bed covers on my side of the bed, sat down, and swung my feet up. Just as I slipped my newly cleansed and lotioned body between the sheets, I heard the unmistakable sound of Virginia Woolf vomiting at the foot of the bed.

CHAPTER 6

Hopewell Junction. Charming country cottage with views of valley, lots of natural light, 2 bedrooms, 1 bath, fireplace, woodstove. Super barn for farmer/horse lover, 20 minutes to town . . .

Sol had circled this ad in the real estate section of that Sunday's *New York Times*. I found the paper where he'd left it, on the floor next to Virginia Woolf's highly aromatic litter box that had been temporarily relocated to the upstairs bathroom. The ad and the litter box both greeted me bright and early Monday morning. I don't know if Sol intended for me to see the ad, but he certainly hadn't hidden it.

Instantly I regretted not having confronted Sol on Sunday. I had let the day go by without telling him how upset I was when I heard from other people of our supposed "plans." Part of me was still in deep denial that my beloved was actually behaving so irrationally. But another reason I hadn't been up for a confrontation was simply that I had a lot of student papers to read and wanted to spend a peaceful Sunday getting them done and preparing for classes. After lounging all Saturday afternoon at the block party, I didn't have enough weekend left for an argument. But one look at that ad and the two or three others he'd circled, and I resolved not to put it off for another minute. My first class wasn't until ten, so I figured we had over two hours to wrangle.

Clutching the paper, I charged downstairs, rehearsing my opening salvo, which was going to be, "Sol, since when do you plan and broadcast major life changes without even consulting me? Right after the terrorist attack, we had one brief conversation about the possibility of leaving the metropolitan area. But we never actually decided to do it. I certainly never agreed to move. I know you were terribly upset by what you witnessed, and I really think you need to talk to somebody about . . ."

But I swallowed my entire speech the minute I reached the bottom flight of stairs. Sol and I couldn't possibly have a discussion, let alone a fight, now. Ed was on the job already, and he and Sol, Styrofoam coffee cups in their hands, were hunched over a set of sketches. Silly me. I'd forgotten that we seldom enjoyed the luxury of privacy in our own home anymore.

"Good morning, Professor. Is this too loud?" I barely registered Ed's good-humored question, let alone the decibel level of the hymns he was listening to. But I nodded because although his inquiry was a rhetorical one, it was a courtesy that I usually appreciated. The mason who had repointed our interior brick wall had sung along with operatic arias that reverberated throughout the house, the plumber and his helper blasted salsa, and the electrician was a hip-hop fan. Ed's preference, inspirational music, seemed tame and muted in comparison, although the hymns sometimes competed with the endless stream of NPR news that Sol had been tuned in to during his every waking moment since September 11.

"Ed bought you some tea," Sol said, pointing to a third Styrofoam cup perched on a carton adjacent to the one they were leaning on.

"It's Soothing Moments, the kind you like," Ed said, a smile lighting up his angular face. "I swear, all my clients should drink this stuff while I'm pullin' apart their houses." He reached a lanky arm across the carton he and Sol were using for a counter, grabbed the cup, and handed it to me. I nodded a second time. If either man had noticed that I had not yet uttered a word, he gave no sign.

"We're going over the sketches for the cabinets," Sol said. He looked enthusiastic about the long-awaited custom cabinets even though, with a chill, I realized he had no plans to use them himself. Maybe Felice was right. Sol probably figured that the spiffy new dream kitchen we could just barely afford would add to the resale value of the house. I wondered what kind of kitchen cabinets the "cottage" in Hopewell Junction boasted.

"Yeah, I figured I'd start framin' 'em while we're waitin' for the plumber and the electrician to come back and install the appliances. That should keep us more or less on schedule," Ed said, flashing me another smile. Reminding myself that none of what was bothering me was Ed's fault, I struggled to find a smile to return. "And I got somebody comin' to haul these away today or tomorrow," he added pointing to our old appliances. "That way we all got a little more room."

"Thanks for the tea, Ed," I said, wondering if Sol had even noticed that I hadn't greeted him. "I'll take it with me. I have an early conference with a student this morning, so I have to get to the college. Here, Sol, you left this on the floor upstairs." I handed him the newspaper.

I didn't stick around to see his reaction. Although I didn't really have an early conference, I knew I'd have more peace and privacy at RECC than at home, and just then I really wanted to be alone. So grabbing my book bag and purse, I said, "Sol, don't forget to put Virginia Woolf upstairs, and, while you're at it, please change the litter box or she won't use it."

"You wanna take this with you, Professor? I brought them both in. I already gave Sol his," said Ed, handing me the *Jersey City Herald*, still wrapped in plastic. "Didn't want some yuppie on his way to catch a train to help hisself to your papers." Clearly pleased with himself for having prevented what was a real and extremely annoying local pattern of theft, Ed pointed at the *New York Times* atop a pile of neatly stacked lumber. In the house for less than an hour, the signature bright blue cylinder was already white with plaster dust.

Stashing the local paper in my book bag, I wound my way through what had been the kitchen and living-dining area to the front door. "Thanks, Ed. I'll read it during lunch. Sol, don't forget about Virginia Woolf, please." I heard the phone ringing as I left the house, but I didn't go back.

The phone was ringing in my office too when I opened the door. Putting down the chocolate croissant I'd treated myself to and the still-warm tea, I answered. "Professor Barrett here. Good morning." I spoke with all the heartiness I could muster.

"Bel, I'm glad I got you. What are you doing at work so early? I just left you a message at home." I recognized Betty's voice. "I'm upstairs in my office. Can I come down for a minute? I want to talk to you."

"Of course," I said, steeling myself to share

my chocolate croissant with my dear friend. "Nobody's here. Come on down. The door's open." I reached behind me and turned the doorknob with my free hand. Betty probably wanted to apologize for not showing up on Saturday, and that was a good sign. Putting the phone down, I hung up my jacket and emptied my book bag, sorting the papers and books by course. I put the newspaper aside, saving it for what I hoped would be a leisurely and uninterrupted lunch.

As I was checking my desk calendar to see what students to expect for conferences, Betty arrived, a newspaper in one hand and a traveling mug of coffee in the other. I was glad to see that my friend's eyes showed traces of their customary gleam. Unlike Sol, perhaps Betty was beginning to recover from the trauma she had experienced. "Want half?" I asked by way of greeting, pointing to the flaky croissant oozing chocolate that I'd picked up in Hoboken. There seemed no better way to reward Betty for beginning to rally.

"Uh, I don't think so, girl, but I really appreciate your offering. Let's face it, we both know you'd never really forgive me if I took half your chocolate croissant." Betty managed a fairly convincing grin and pulled a paper bag out of her purse. "Anyway, I've got a corn muffin here, so don't sweat it. Go ahead, enjoy."

"So you stood us up on Saturday," I said, introducing what I thought was the topic she'd stopped in to discuss.

"Yeah, but that's besides the point," Betty said, breaking her muffin in half. "You haven't read this morning's paper yet, have you?" she asked, eyeing the still-wrapped newspaper on my desk. "I hate to be the one to break this to you, Bel, but I didn't want you to hear it from the students or, God forbid, Woodman." Betty winced as she named her boss, RECC's president. "I swear, girl that man is fit to be tied what with all the reporters calling him at home yesterday. Damn if he didn't give them my number and let them intrude on my Sunday." Betty's voice was low, serious.

"Is it our accreditation? Are we on probationary status again? Is that it?" I asked, struggling to imagine anything that would rouse reporters to pay attention to RECC what with all the rescue work and memorial services to cover.

"Bel, that adjunct you have in your seminar, the one you helped to get an apartment on your block? Eunice Goodson?" I nodded, somehow not wanting to hear the rest.

"Bel, she's dead," said Betty.

"What? I just saw her on Saturday. She was fine," I said, the croissant having suddenly turned to Styrofoam between my teeth. It was all I could do not to retch. "She came to the block party and then she left for her other job." As I spoke I could once again see Eunice's small figure receding down the street. "That's impossible," I said, reflexively.

"I knew you were going to say that," said Betty, "so I brought this." As she spoke, Betty unfolded the *Jersey City Herald* she had carried in with her and placed it on my desk, front page facing me. "See for yourself."

CHAPTER 7

CLUB GIRL FOUND DEAD
TAUGHT ANATOMY AT RECC

The body of Eunice Goodson, 28, of Hoboken was found at 6:25 on Sunday morning in the plaza adjacent to the Erie Lackawanna Railroad Terminal in Hoboken. An exotic dancer who performed at Manhattan's the Big Apple Peel, Goodson also taught anatomy at River Edge Community College. Her landlord, Felice Aquino, said Goodson was originally from upstate New York and had only recently relocated to New Jersey. According to Aquino, "I knew she was a professor. I had no idea she was a dancer too, but no matter. She was a model tenant. I can't imagine why anybody would hurt her." Elizabeth Ramsey, spokesperson for RECC President Ron Woodman said, "President Woodman extends his heartfelt condolences to Ms. Goodson's family." Apparently accosted on her way home from work, Goodson appears to have suffered a chest wound. Her death is being investigated.

My hand trembled as I reached for the paper. I held it at arm's length and scanned the column of print and then, propping my reading glasses on the end of my nose, reread the lead article. Betty sat quietly sipping her coffee.

"You know, I was worried about her coming home from that job of hers by herself at all hours, but . . ." I felt tears forming and reached for a Kleenex. Lately there had been a steady stream of weeping students in my office, so I'd replaced the Kleenex box twice since this ill-fated semester began. Now my own tears were flowing. "She was such a smart, nice young woman. I can't imagine anybody who'd want to hurt Eunice Goodson, let alone kill her," I said, snuffling into the tissue and reaching for another one. "It must have been a robbery or maybe some perverted fan," I speculated, once again wishing I had admonished her about traveling back to Hoboken alone after work. I struggled to fend off a wave of guilt. "Who's taking over her classes?" Veteran prof that I am, I was also concerned about Eunice's students.

"No one yet, but I called Nigar Hasgam, her department chair, and Nigar's going to find somebody or do it herself. That's what department chairs are for, so it's not your problem and it's not your fault," said Betty giving me a knowing look designed to wither

75

any guilt I might have assumed. "And the cops have notified Eunice's family, I'm sure," she added. "So there's nothing for you to do, not this time." I could tell Betty was trying to reassure me, no doubt remembering when I'd had to take over Vinny Vallone's class after his death. "But since she was in your seminar and you were getting to know her, I thought I'd tell you about it myself . . . and . . ." Between my sniffles, I detected Betty's very slight hesitation.

"And what?" I asked, somewhat mechanically. I could hear the dullness in my voice. Nothing would surprise me now. This was surely the semester from hell. Hadn't we all had enough death?

"Woodman is on another rampage," Betty said matter-of-factly. Normally Ron Woodman was, if not exactly reasonable, at least quite manageable, but every once in a while, he lost it, and then Betty had her hands full trying to talk him back into his usual state of docile malleability. "Come to think of it, lately he's been in his wild-man mode a lot. The man's a candidate for some kind of mood-altering meds, I swear. Hmmm . . ."

"Let me guess. He's upset because a faculty member was murdered and that's bad press for RECC," I said. "Remember when Belinda Judd was killed and all he could think of was how the trustees would react to

76

the bad press?" I asked, disgust twisting my lips into a sneer.

"Well, Bel, the Judd girl was a student and another student was a suspect. You have to admit it didn't look very good for the college," said Betty. I didn't know whether to be glad she was sounding more like her old self or mad because that self was sometimes so pragmatic as to seem insensitive. "How *do* you suppose the trustees are going to react to the news that we had a stripper on the faculty?"

I blinked. Betty's perfectly logical question took me by surprise. "What difference does that make?" I sputtered, balling up my latest Kleenex and adding it to the pile of little white blobs accumulating on my desk. "That's really none of Woodman's business. And it's none of the trustees' business either," I added, anticipating Betty's next comment. Really annoyed at the puritanical pettiness of RECC's president, I swept the wads of Kleenex into the basket as if with that gesture I could sweep away those who would question the integrity or professionalism of Eunice Goodson. "My God, RECC didn't pay her enough to live on, so she had to do something else. And she had the stuff it takes to be a super teacher. That's really all she ever wanted to do."

"Don't argue with *me*, Bel, I'm just telling you what's on our leader's mind before . . ."

This time Betty's hesitation was prolonged enough to be obvious.

"Before what?" I asked, grief and anger making my voice sharp.

"Before Woodman calls you in for a chat. He's gotten it into his head from something the landlady said that you knew Eunice Goodson was a stripper and didn't tell anybody. If you'd told Nigar, Nigar would've told Wooodman and Woodman would have ordered Nigar to fire Goodson," Betty explained. At least she had the sense to look sheepish as she tried to explicate her boss's loopy logic.

"And then Goodson could have sued the place for discrimination of all kinds and I would have supported her," I said quietly. "It must be hard to have to work directly with somebody so shortsighted." Privately I congratulated myself for having edited the word "stupid" out of that sentence before it left my mouth. "Betty, doesn't Woodman realize that the McCarthy era is over?"

"I don't know, girl. I don't know." Betty's disclaimer came out as a prolonged sigh. "Why don't you just ask him that when you talk to him?"

"Right," I said, suddenly eager to change the subject. "So tell me, why didn't you and Vic come to the block party? We missed you."

"We thought about it, but Vic had a funeral on Saturday morning and we just didn't have much energy left after that. He's looking at a really hard time coming up," Betty said, referring, no doubt to the scores of Jersey City folks killed by the terrorists. "It's not like you're burying old folks or sick folks or even soldiers." She thought for a minute and added, "In fact, it's not like you're burying anybody."

"I know." Terrorism had been bad for every business, even Vic's. With no corpses to embalm or bury, many funerals had become memorial services, better suited to the church, mosque, or synagogue than to the funeral home. "But I'm doing better," Betty said, trying to reassure both of us. "How's Sol?"

Now it was my turn to sigh. "Not great." For a moment I marveled at how this phrase had become the euphemism of choice for responding to this well-meant inquiry. But I didn't need to use euphemisms when talking to Betty. "Actually, since you ask, he's still upset. In fact, he's started telling the neighbors and even my mother, for God's sake, that we're moving to the country." Betty's eyes widened, but she let me finish. "He's circling ads for houses in the boonies. I've got to get him to talk to somebody."

"Have you talked to him, yet?" Once again I was blind-sided by Betty's logic. Why was I trying to get Sol to talk to a shrink about his

79

state of mind and his plans when I hadn't made the time to sit down with him and hash things out? We'd always been able to talk through our worries and disagreements before. In fact, one of the things I loved most about Sol was that he was able to go head-to-head with me. We'd always emerged from these sessions with our bond renewed and closer than ever. So why was I avoiding this particular conversation?

"Good question," I finally replied. "Thanks for asking it. I'll think on it. And thanks for letting me know about Eunice too."

"I'm just glad you didn't shoot the messenger," said Betty, standing and brushing muffin crumbs from the front of her pale yellow sweater set and gray slacks.

"Not this time," I said, trying to lighten up before we parted. "But if you can't whip Woodman into shape before he calls me on the only carpet in the college, I may have to." We both managed a smile at my not so subtle reference to the fact that the only carpeting to be found anywhere at RECC graced the floor of the presidential suite.

"I'll do my best," Betty promised as she left my office, taking her newspaper with her.

Ron Woodman had wasted no time summoning me to an audience right after my late-afternoon class. Dutifully I made my way to the "Penthouse," which is how RECC students and faculty refer to the president's office. I'm

80

not sure whether we call it that because of its location on the building's fourteenth floor or its opulence relative to the rest of the college.

When I got there, Betty winked and ushered me into the inner sanctum where, as usual, Woodman waited at his desk beneath portraits of members of the Board of Trustees. Unlike the faces in this gallery of local rogues, Ron Woodman's face looked haggard. New lines creased his forehead and extended the corners of his mouth. The black fringe circling his scalp was flecked with gray, and there was less of it than I recalled. He had aged, but then, I reminded myself, so had we all. I steeled myself for the presidential reprimand Betty had warned me about.

"Bel, thanks for coming so promptly. How are you? I haven't talked to you since . . ." he paused and nodded at the window, where in the distance the abruptly abbreviated Manhattan skyline completed his sentence for him. No wonder the poor man looked somewhat the worse for wear. From his desk he had had an unobstructed view of the Twin Towers just across the Hudson about a mile away. In prior conversations, Woodman had always glanced over his shoulder at the likenesses of the trustees glowering down from the wall behind him as if to beg them to approve of whatever petty or momentous decision he had to make. Was it possible that his frame of reference had shifted? Could it be that forces far darker and even more powerful than RECC's trustees had seized his attention and reordered his priorities? Before I got too carried away with this possibility, I remembered Betty's account of Woodman's reaction to Eunice's death.

"I'm fine, thanks," I replied stiffly, wary of being caught off guard. "And you?" I asked, struggling to be civil while confronting the results of the cataclysm just past and anticipating the castigation to come.

"Well, Bel, just between you and me, thanks to these, I'm feeling a little better," he said, pulling a small bottle out of his pocket and putting it on the desk. "They're anti-anxiety pills and they really work." In spite of my resolve to be prepared for whatever Woodman dished out, this particular personal moment of show-and-tell took me aback. I suppressed a smile, realizing that Betty had probably persuaded her boss to try chemical intervention. No wonder she had winked at me when I arrived. Woodman seemed unaware of my amusement as, pocketing his pill bottle, he continued. "So tell me, Bel, how are our students doing in the aftermath of September 11? I can always count on you to be in touch with the student sensibility," he said, leaning back in his chair and waiting for me to respond.

"Well, actually, most of them are doing very well, considering," I said. Then, warming to the subject, I went on, "But two of my Pakistani students have withdrawn. They're brothers living with relatives here, and their parents want them to come home." Woodman's eyebrows arched in a question. "Their parents don't think the boys are safe in the U.S. now," I explained as patiently as I could, wondering how this seemingly obvious fact could elude a college president. "And I have one Lebanese student who is changing his name from Mohammad Aziz to Michael Atkins. He thinks he'll be less likely to attract negative attention that way," I said, remembering a generation ago when my own ancestors had anglicized their Jewish names for similar reasons. "But one way or another, most of my students are coping. Even those who lost relatives or jobs are struggling to pick up the pieces and get on with their education," I said, as always pleased to report on the resiliency and determination of RECC students.

"Well, I'm glad to hear that. I really am," Woodman said, leaning forward now. Just as I began to marvel at what might be in the pills the man was popping to bring about this rare show of concern for our students, Woodman spoke again, "And I know that you and the rest of the faculty are doing everything you can to help them?" Once more I marveled.

What miracle med was he on? Whatever the elixir was, it had prompted Ron Woodman to articulate his appreciation for the RECC faculty, something else he very seldom did. "That's why I almost hate to ask you to take on anything else, Bel, but . . ." he paused and looked behind him, not at the trustees now, but at the altered skyline.

As if somehow fortified by the view, he stiffened his shoulders and continued. "I know that you were upset by Eunice Goodson's death, Bel. She was taking your seminar and, I understand, she was your neighbor as well." Even before Woodman paused this time, I braced myself for the reprimand Betty had prepared me for. I was so busy wording a self-righteous rebuttal defending Eunice's right to privacy as well as her right to supplement her paltry adjunct's pay by any legal means available to her that I almost missed Woodman's next words. "Bel, would you look into the question of her death?"

For the fourth time in a single conversation, I was flabbergasted. Fortunately Woodman hadn't finished his pitch, so I didn't have to respond immediately. "We both know that you have quite a successful track record at this sort of thing. And we both know the police aren't going to have time to give the murder of an out-of-town club girl their full attention anytime soon.

84

And we both know that the Gang of Twelve," Woodman jerked his head behind him, a plain and newly irreverent reference to the trustees, "well, they're pretty upset, not only that the woman was killed but also that someone on our faculty was an exotic dancer." He shrugged his shoulders as if to minimize the trustees' concern. If I weren't already in a state of shock, Woodman's flip references to the trustees would have rendered me speechless.

Again I was spared having to reply because the president had not yet finished what was clearly a well-rehearsed plea. "And, Bel, we both know RECC didn't need another murder, especially this year. And we don't need any more scandals either. So I figure the sooner this gets cleared up and out of the papers, the better for everybody, right?" Woodman signaled that he had come to the end of his spiel by smiling a smile that was a bit too perky. Leaning back in his chair, he awaited my response.

Now that the ball had finally landed in my court, I didn't know what to do with it. I wasn't at all sure I had what it took to look into Eunice's murder, probably the act of some sicko fan of hers. But if I did agree to poke around, I wanted to be sure I had Betty and Illuminada's blessing and backup before I made any promises. And I'd have to see where Sol stood too. "I'll have to think about

85

it, Ron," I stammered. "I'll think it over and get back to you." I stood and left his office, rolling my eyes at Betty as I passed her desk on my way to the elevator.

CHAPTER 8

To: Bbarrett@circle.com
From: Rbarrett@uwash.edu
Re: Sol's meltdown
Date: 10/22/01 18:05:37

Mom,

Is Sol going through male menopause (again) or what? He actually e-mailed asking me to help him convince you to retire early so the two of you can move to some little house in the country. What is that dude thinking, Mom? I know he saw the whole WTC horror from the ferry, but I had no idea how traumatized he was.

I just can't picture you leaving teaching. It's what you do. If you didn't have your students and their papers, ohmigod . . . well, you'd be somebody else. And leaving Hoboken to live in the Hudson River Valley near *his* daughter? Hel-lo, Sol. I e-mailed him back that if you were going to retire early, you'd move out here so you could be close to your own daughter and your own granddaughter. Then I wouldn't have to take Abbie J to day care and Keith and

I could save all kinds of money. Wouldn't that be awesome? But you're never going to retire, are you?

I sure hope Sol feels better soon.

Love,
Rebecca

There was no time to respond to Rebecca's disturbing e-mail, so, I printed it out and stuffed it into my purse to reread when I had a minute. Then I left for Betty's house to meet with her and Illuminada. I stopped on the way for some brie, apple, and smoked turkey roll-ups and a six-pack of Amstel Lite. We gathered around Betty's coffee table, leaning over to avoid getting sandwich droppings on her immaculate carpet. As had become my habit, I now eyed my friend's orderly and clean home with barely disguised envy. "So, *chiquita*, did you get us over here tonight to deprive us of our beauty sleep, ruin our domestic lives, or just because you felt like a picnic?" Illuminada asked not long after we had started our sandwiches.

"None of the above," I replied, sipping a beer. "It's about Eunice Goodson, the adjunct who was murdered. You must have read about it in the paper."

"Right. The stripper," said Illuminada with no inflection at all. "Betty mentioned it. She was the one taking your seminar, the one you got the apartment for, right?"

"Right," I answered, admiring my friend's memory. "In one of her most inspired and long overdue feats of mind control yet, our own Betty has put President Woodman on psychotropic meds. His entire personality has been reconfigured. He's been born again as a civil, student-friendly, and profaculty pragmatist!" I couldn't help giggling about halfway through this proclamation, and that rather diminished its impact.

"*Dios mío*, Bel," said Illuminada. "Unlike you, I have a clean and welcoming home waiting for me. I'd like to get back there this evening. What does Ron Woodman's drug intake have to do with Eunice Goodson's death and what do either of these things have to do with us?"

I was used to Illuminada's impatience just as she was used to my attenuated-narrative style, so I ignored her dig. But I did get to the point. "Woodman actually asked me to figure out who killed Eunice. He assumes the cops are too busy now to do it right. And the trustees, of course, are upset. They're upset not only by the fact that the poor woman is dead, but also by the revelation that she was a stripper, right?" I turned to Betty for confirmation of my summary thus far.

"You got it. But the new Woodman is not quivering in his boots over the trustees like he used to be. Rather the dude is trying to solve what he sees as a legitimate administrative problem," Betty said, twisting open her beer. "Of course, what he sees as a legitimate administrative problem is what I tell him," she added, lowering her eyes in mock modesty. "Those pills may have calmed him down, but they sure haven't made him smarter." She shook her head at her boss's familiar limitations.

"So, do you want to?" asked Illuminada, crumpling up her empty sandwich wrapper in her dainty fist.

"I think so. I really liked Eunice. And I don't like the idea of some sicko out there preying on young women. But I'm just not so sure where to start. I mean what do I know about strip clubs? And then there's Sol," I added, my voice lowered.

"How comfortable will he be with your taking on this one?" asked Illuminada. It had become almost a ritual to check Sol's state of mind about my participation in any investigation ever since he had almost left me when I tried to find Vinny Vallone's killer.

"I don't know. I'll ask him," I answered. "We're long overdue for a chat anyway. I'll talk to him and I'll get back to you." As if to signal that this particular soiree was over, I picked up a few dead soldiers and sandwich wrappers and carried them into the kitchen, noting as I dumped the wrappers that even Betty's trash looked clean and well organized.

The following afternoon after work I was waiting for Sol to come home so I could talk with him about, among other things, my taking on another murder investigation. I had not even figured out how to approach him when he burst into the bedroom, still the only relatively noise- and filth-free room in the house. My neck muscles tensed when I heard the urgent undertone in his deep voice. "Bel, we've got to help Charlie. He grabbed me as I was getting out of the car. The poor guy's been sitting on his stoop waiting for me."

"What's wrong? Is Ilona okay? Is it her sugar?" Ilona had fainted on the street twice over the summer, and those of us who knew about these episodes were concerned that her diabetes was worsening. "Or is it Yronellis?" I asked.

Sol nodded, giving me a cursory hug and pulling me down to sit beside him on the bed. "It's Yronellis. The cops want to question her."

"Why? She doesn't even drive," I asked, recalling my son's numerous run-ins with the local police when he was Yronellis's age and a newly licensed driver. "And she's always studying. I doubt if she drinks or even dates," I added, remembering the missed curfews and transparent excuses that had punctuated my own daughter's late teens. Any infraction the studious and sheltered Yronellis might be capable of would seem tame in comparison with the youthful exploits of my own children. I was unprepared for Sol's response.

"No. It's nothing like that. The cops suspect Yronellis of killing your friend Eunice Goodson." Sol paused, giving me a chance to absorb his truly startling revelation.

I stood and whirled to face him. "What? Why on earth would they suspect her? She's not exactly personality plus, but Yronellis would never kill anybody. They must have other much more likely suspects."

"Well, don't yell at me," Sol said, standing to face me, eyeball to eyeball in the crowded bedroom that had suddenly become a cage. The only way we could talk facing each other was to lie down on the bed or stand up. At another time, our predicament might have seemed ludicrous. That afternoon it was maddening. Sharing my frustration, Sol lifted some boxes off the chair near the window and balanced them atop the other cartons already stacked in the corner. I pulled the chair around to face the bed. "You can sit down," he said, pointing at the chair. I sat and he resumed his seat now opposite me on the edge of the bed. Then he continued, "Don't blame me. It's not my fault the cops are questioning the Illysario kid."

Suddenly our voices were amplified by an unaccustomed silence. Ed had turned off the sander for a blessed moment. Sol and I stopped talking to savor a few seconds of stillness when we heard Ed's voice accompanying his knock on our bedroom door. "Professor? Sol? You got a minute?"

"Yeah," said Sol, his monosyllabic response more a resigned exhalation than an assent. "Come on in. What's up?" The question was intended as much to atone for his initial pique as to satisfy his curiosity.

"I'm afraid I got some bad news for ya." Ed's apologetic tone was the preface to another delay. I braced myself, and I could feel Sol tense. Our knees touched as if to support one another through the latest setback. "Enrico, the guy who's gonna do the drillin', you know, for the floor-through AC units? Well, his wife's havin' a baby down in Elizabeth. He called me from the hospital. He'll be here tomorrow mornin' first thing though. I made him swear." Ed smiled. Sol and I shrugged in unison, helpless to avert the most recent postponement. His bad news dutifully dispatched, Ed left, closing the bedroom door behind him, and in a few seconds we once again heard the rasp of the sander.

"Bel, I promised Charlie and Ilona that you would talk to them. That's why Charlie was waiting for me. The poor guy felt funny going to you without talking to me first, you know?" I knew. Like many men with Old-World sensibilities, Charlie still felt he had to get the male half of a couple's okay before

93

approaching the female half for a favor. If Charlie had only known how the inherent sexism in this oblique foreplay imitated me, he would have tried another way to get my attention. Sol read my mind. "Oh come off it, Bel. We're not talking feminist protocol here. This is Charlie Illysario, remember? He's been your neighbor for over twenty years and his kid's in trouble."

Sol was right. Distracted from his anxiety, he was behaving more like his pre–September 11 self, and Sol's pre–September 11 self had been right about a lot of things. I allowed myself to hope that, with help, Sol might eventually recover from his post-traumatic stress disorder. With that sustaining thought, I stood, planted a kiss on his thinning hair, and said, "I'm sorry. Of course, you're right. Why don't we go over there right now and talk to Ilona and Charlie? They must be frantic." As I spoke, I wondered if Ron Woodman had asked me to investigate Eunice's murder because he already knew that Illysario, a RECC student, was a suspect.

The first thing I noticed after entering the Illysarios' living room was not the stricken looks on Yronellis's and Ilona's tear-stained faces or the pallor of Charlie's but rather how clean, orderly, and quiet their home was compared to the hellhole Sol and I had just left. "Bel, thank you. I told Ilona I knew you'd help us," said Charlie, motioning us to have a seat. Contemplating the pristine beige sofa, I brushed off my skirt before sitting.

"Yeah. We're countin' on you, Bel. Our lawyer said to keep our fingers crossed, but that's not good enough," Ilona said. "Not when it comes to my daughter." Ilona was stroking Yronellis's hair as she continued. "See, Bel. We told Ronni we'd take care of this. She has an exam tomorrow, poor kid. I don't want her losing her focus, you know?" said Ilona, removing her hand from Yronellis's hair to tug at an orange tuft of her own that looked as if it had been tugged at before. Ilona's usually hearty voice sounded tentative, as if she had lost her own focus.

I nodded and said, "I'm sure the police must have other suspects, so their questioning of Yronellis may be merely routine." I noted that Ilona was not plying us with tea or coffee, a very bad sign. Ilona was notorious for her aggressive approach to hospitality.

"The police," Charlie said, shrugging his shoulders and opening his palms in a gesture of hopelessness. "Those poor bastards are all workin' overtime followin' up anthrax scares and bomb scares and monitorin' Lincoln Tunnel traffic. They don't got time to do their regular work. My girl is an easy arrest because they think she's got a motive," he said, his voice getting lower and lower so that by the end of this lament, he was whispering.

"What motive could you possibly have for

wanting to kill Eunice Goodson?" I asked, speaking directly to Yronellis. When she said nothing but began to chew on the cuticle of her thumb, I leaned closer to Charlie in the hope of catching his response.

This effort proved unnecessary because before he could open his mouth, Ilona blurted out the answer to my question. "They think she did it because of the PANA scholarship, Bel."

Suddenly I sensed where this was going and the realization chilled me. "Tell me more," I said, turning toward Ilona. I hoped her next words would prove me wrong.

"You brought that woman here, Bel, into our neighborhood, into PANA." Her tone was accusatory. "You got Felice to rent her an apartment. Next thing we knew, she was on the Scholarship Committee." Ilona paused, glaring at me. "I happen to know it was her, a total stranger, who kept our Ronni from getting that scholarship." Now Ilona's voice was low. She knew she wasn't supposed to have heard what had transpired at the meeting of the Scholarship Committee. And she had probably promised Tony or Joey P or Delphine she'd never tell anyone that she did know, especially me. But the accusation of Yronellis had changed the rules.

"That's all true," I said, resolving on the spot to resign from the PANA Scholarship Committee, which I now saw as a hotbed of intrigue. "But it's absurd to think that Yronellis would murder someone for that scholarship." I glanced over at Yronellis, now chewing on the cuticle of her index finger, still silent beside her mother at the table. I flashed the poor girl what I hoped was a comforting smile and said, "She's not perfect, but she's not a killer."

Charlie's eyes widened at my assertion that Yronellis was not perfect, but he did not address that when he next spoke. What he did say was "Okay, Bel, so will you find out who killed that woman? You know you always get to the bottom of these things and the cops are too busy. We don't want our girl to suffer no more."

Before I could formulate a response, Ilona spoke. Her voice was shrill with tension and her words a sharp contrast to her husband's polite request. "Look, Bel, if it wasn't for you, my daughter would have another scholarship, not be fightin' a murder rap." Ilona's voice cracked as she continued. "You just gotta find out who really did kill that slut."

"I'll do what I can, Ilona," I said, struggling to stifle the urge to slap my neighbor silly for badmouthing my dead friend. I knew Ilona was worried about her daughter, but that was hardly an excuse for slandering Eunice. I signaled to Sol that I was ready to leave. I wanted to get out of there before I made a bad matter worse.

CHAPTER 9

To: Bbarrett@circle.com
From: Mbarrett@hotmail.com
Re: Sol
Date: 10/24/01 08:19:16

Yo Ma Bel,

Just got this really way out there e-mail
from Sol asking me to try to talk you
into retiring early and moving to the
country in case there's another attack in
the metropolitan area. Is this the same
dude who routinely flew to Eastern Eu-
rope in the middle of a war to spread
democracy and dollars? He sounds like
he's had a major brain slam. Besides, *my*
mom would never give up teaching.
Anyway you're not old enough to retire.
And let's get real, you would never live
more than a block from Marie's Brick
Oven Bakery, right? Hoboken rocks, man.
Anyway if you moved, I'd have to put all
the stuff I still have in my room in
storage. The whole idea is totally lame.
But I guess Sol's rattled by what happened (like who isn't?), so I'll cut him

some slack when I answer. The dude just needs a little time.

Everything's cool here in Maine. I mean really cool, like winter.

Love,
Mark

Scanning Mark's e-mail the morning after our visit to the Illysarios, I remembered the one from Rebecca that I had barely read, let alone responded to. Quickly I printed Mark's message and filed it in my purse with his sister's. With any luck at all, I'd have a few minutes between classes to e-mail my children, although exactly what I could say to reassure them was not at all clear to me as I drove to work that morning. Nor was there time to think about it then. I was too busy processing my conversation with the Illysarios. Betty and Illuminada were both waiting at my office door when I got there.

Illuminada forced a buttered bagel into my hand, and Betty pointed to a cup of tea waiting on my desk. "*Dios mío, chiquita,* you sounded so rushed when you called this morning we were afraid you'd forget to stop," said Illuminada. "And then we'd have to deal with your empty stomach." She grimaced at the thought of how nasty I got when I was hungry and then took a call that came in on her cell phone.

"So, girlfriend, what's happening? I've got a

meeting at nine," Betty said, taking her turn at watching the clock. She perched on my office mate's desk, and Illuminada took the vacant chair. It was a good thing Wendy didn't come in until her ten o'clock class. I made the time-out sign, sat at my desk, and devoured half of the bagel while Illuminada chattered in Spanish. When she had finished, I announced, "The cops are questioning Yronellis Illysario."

Silence greeted my pronouncement. Then Betty spoke. "Who the hell is Yronellis Whatevero?"

"She's a RECC student who lives down the street from me. She's a nice enough kid, a little sheltered by her overly protective parents, but hardworking and ambitious," I explained. Directing my next comment to Illuminada, who had started tapping her watch, I added. "Remember, you saw her at the mike at the PANA block party? The kid with the platform shoes and the designer jeans? Remember? Last year she won the PANA Scholarship."

Illuminada looked blank and shrugged. She said, "Skip the bio, Bel. I don't remember her. I was probably filling my plate when she did her thing. And why on earth are we talking about her problems with the police anyway?" Illuminada didn't have to tap her watch now. Her voice had an edge to it and I knew she was losing what little patience she had.

"The cops think she might have killed Eunice Goodson," I said, taking enormous pleasure in watching both of my friends' mouths open in near unison.

Betty was the first to react. "I don't think Woodman has a clue that they suspect a student. I may have to get the doctor to increase his dose when he and the trustees find that out."

"*Dios mío,* they must have something on her," Illuminada said. "Is this kid a stripper too? Was there maybe a turf war over tips? There had to be something. Will she talk to you?" Illuminada asked.

"No, she's not a stripper," I said with assurance. "The cops think Yronellis was angry at Eunice because of the PANA Scholarship." Both Betty and Illuminada opened their mouths to protest this absurd notion, even as I hastened to explain. "Eunice was on the scholarship committee and we decided not to award the grant to Yronellis twice in a row. Eunice was a key player in bringing that about. And even though committee meetings are confidential, I guess the members don't always take that too seriously, which is why the Illysarios know everything Eunice said and did at that meeting?"

Illuminada was shaking her head. "The cops have to have something that really connects Yronellis to that murder," she insisted.

"Didn't the family say what it was while you were there?"

"They probably would have, but I got so angry when her mother called Eunice a slut that I didn't stay to ask," I recounted. "Mea culpa," I added quickly, eager to acknowledge my blooper before Betty and Illuminada got on me about it.

I knew that ploy had failed when Illuminada said, "You left before you asked about that?" Her tone was as close to scathing as you can get with a mouthful of bagel.

"What did you expect, Bel? It's hard to behave like Miss Manners when you're worried about your kid," said Betty, who had had a fair amount of practice worrying about Randy even before September 11.

"I know, I know. I was tired and I lost it," I said. "So I pleaded an appointment, and we left. I figured it was better to exit before I said something equally insulting to her. But before we walked out the door, I asked Yronellis to come see me this morning."

"Good rescue, girlfriend," said Betty flashing me a smile.

Illuminada nodded her approval and said, "I'll try to get a police report as well. There will be an autopsy, I'm sure."

"Thanks," I said. Then I paused a moment and added, "You know what? The really good news about this whole mess is that Sol is really hot for us to gel Yronellis exonerated. Charlie, Tony, and Joey P have been having breakfast together once a month ever since Charlie retired, and Sol goes too. He's gotten pretty close to Charlie," I said.

"I'm just glad Sol's not going to give you a hard time," said Illuminada.

"Me too. And it'll be really good for him to be involved. It will draw him even closer to our neighborhood, and then maybe he'll get over wanting to move out of the metropolitan area," I said. "His deep sense of connection will make him feel safe here."

Betty began humming the theme from *Mr. Rogers' Neighborhood.*

But it was Illuminada who had the last word. "*Chiquita,* once you get involved with the seedy lowlifes in the New York sex trade, Sol may want you to move to the country pronto." In case I missed her point, she snapped her fingers in my face as she spoke the last word. Then she stood and drew her car keys out of her purse. "Later," she said as she left my office to begin her own workday.

Before I had time to wonder if Yronellis was going to show up, she knocked on the door to my office. I leaned back in my chair and opened it. "Come on in and sit down," I said, pointing to Wendy's chair. Yronellis sat down, inserted her index finger in her mouth, and began to chew on the cuticle. Up close,

I saw that her nails were oases of gleaming enamel surrounded by raw, ragged flesh. The poor kid was eating herself alive. "I'm glad you came, Yronellis," I said. She nodded. Fighting the urge to remove her hand from her mouth, I added, "I'd like to help you sort this out."

"Thanks, Professor Barrett," she said. "I need all the help I can get."

"Sol and I are both worried about you. We know you didn't kill Eunice even if you did blame her for not awarding you the PANA Scholarship this year. But there must be some reason for the police to suspect you. What do they have on you?"

Yronellis sat on the hand she had been cannibalizing and raised her eyes to meet mine. "Remember the girl who was hanging out with me and my nephews on my stoop at the block party? My girlfriend Maricel with the black hair?"

"Yes. You two were doing each other's nails, right?" I answered her question with one of my own.

Yronellis nodded. "Well, I was pretty steamed when I didn't get the PANA Scholarship. 'Specially when I heard that it was on accounta that friend of yours, that professor, who gave it to that yuppie." Taking a deep breath, Yronellis continued. "Well, I was talking to Maricel, you know, on the stoop, and I said something I guess I shouldn'a said." Yronellis paused.

When she resumed speaking her voice was low. "I said as how I woulda gotten the money if it wasn't for that bitch in 311 and then I said as how I was gonna find a way to make the bitch pay." As I processed this information, I reminded myself that people in Hoboken often referred to their neighbors by their addresses and Eunice had lived at number 311 Park Avenue. With another deep breath, Yronellis lowered her tear-filled eyes and removed her hand from beneath her and went to work on her finger again.

"Well, you were angry. How were you to know that Professor Goodson would actually be murdered?" I asked, fighting the urge to lecture the poor girl on the foolishness of making threatening statements in front of witnesses. Yronellis was pretty smart, and she sounded as if she had figured that out for herself already. "But what I want to know, Yronellis, is how the police learned that you made that statement."

Grabbing one wrist in the other hand and pulling it down and holding it in her lap, Yronellis resumed speaking. "When Maricel heard about Professor Goodson's murder, she told her sister what I had said. Her sister said Maricel had a 'moral obligation' to tell the cops." Yronellis made the words *moral obligation* sound like an STD. "Can you believe that? So she went down there and told them," said Yronellis, disbelief suddenly animating her voice. "And then, you know what? Maricel actually called me up and told me what she had done. She said how she was sorry but her conscience was clear now." Yronellis uttered the final five words of this sentence in a high-pitched whine, which I took to be an imitation of her friend's declaration.

"But if you'll excuse me, Bel, that's all bullshit." Now Yronellis's eyes narrowed and flashed and suddenly she looked like her mother had looked the night before. "Maricel and I have been friends since we were freshmen in high school. But I made the honor society. She didn't. I got picked to represent St. Fran's at the model United Nations. She didn't. Then I was salutatorian. She wasn't even in the top ten of our class." Yronellis ticked off each of her accomplishments on her fingers and then wedged her hand beneath her seat. "And now I'm in college. And Maricel's loading trucks at UPS. I thought she was my friend, but now I see she's nothing but a jealous bitch." Yronellis spoke with all the self-righteousness of the betrayed adolescent she was. Her speech over, she extricated her hand and began to fiddle with the strap of her shoulder bag. I was relieved that she was giving her poor fingers a respite.

"Well, that certainly explains why the police are questioning you," I said. "Where were you the night Eunice was murdered? After the block party?"

Yronellis abandoned the strap of her purse and this time sat on both hands before she answered. "That's what my lawyer kept askin' me. I was baby-sittin' Ricky and José Jr., my sister's kids, all weekend. She and her husband went to the Poconos for their anniversary." She paused and fidgeted on her chair. Settling down again, she continued. "At about nine I took the kids back uptown to their house and put them to bed. I watched TV for a while and then I went to bed in my sister and brother-in-law's room. I never left that house till the next morning when I took the boys to church and brought them back to my house to eat. My mother and father took them then so I could study." She looked at me, a trace of defiance in her eyes. It was not exactly a watertight alibi and she knew it.

"Okay," I said. "Yronellis, I believe you. I can't promise anything, but I'll give it my best shot. There have to be some other suspects."

CHAPTER 10

To: Bbarrett@circle.com
From: Nvandergast@earthlink.net
Re: My eulogy for Eunice
Date: 1/25/01 10:44:23

Hi Professor Barrett,

I was saddened to learn of the death of our colleague Eunice Goodson. As you know she was my writing partner in the Faculty Development Seminar and I will miss her. I learned there will be no funeral in Jersey City, so I am writing a eulogy for her. With your permission I would like to read it when the seminar meets next as a way of paying our respects to Eunice.

I printed out Nelson's message so I could think about it later. I am not proud of my immediate reaction to Nelson's request, which was *What can a tour guide of Soprano locations possibly have to say about Eunice?* Chastising myself for my snobbery, I added Nelson's request to my stash of printouts, several of them messages from my kids. A quick glance at Rebecca and Mark's recent e-mail only strengthened my resolve to talk with Sol ASAP.

Unfortunately that wasn't going to be very soon because according to Ed, Sol had left for a couple of days to baby-sit for his granddaughter in upstate New York, a chore he performed enthusiastically, often, and sometimes on very short notice. "Yeah, Professor, she called this afternoon and he was outta here in about fifteen minutes. He said you could reach him up there if you need to, and he'll call and let you know when he'll be back," reported Ed, sweeping sawdust and bits of wood into a pile. Absorbing the information he gave me, I stood by while Ed shoveled the sweepings into a plastic bag and twisted the top of the bag into a knot.

Before I had a chance to get too miffed at Sol for leaving at the start of an investigation he had actually encouraged me to take on, Ed continued. "You got a bunch of phone messages too. They're on the machine. And Felice stopped by. She wants you to call her." I bet she did. After all, thanks to me, Felice was not only out a tenant but also involved with a tabloid-ready police investigation. Ed looked around, surveying the wrecked room, and, before I could thank him, he too was out the door. "Your mail's in the foyer," he called over his shoulder. "See ya tomorrow." Ed hadn't mentioned Eunice's murder, and I certainly hadn't felt like passing on more sad news. Like most of the neighbors, he hadn't really had a chance to get to know her, so her death could hardly be expected to be of more than superficial interest, especially with so many others to mourn already.

I called Felice at home and at her shop, leaving messages in both places. When she called back, I was standing between two waist-high cartons trying to visualize the sleek custom cabinets Ed, Sol, and I had so painstakingly designed. "Bel, I know you've heard about Eunice by now. We need to talk." I recognized an undertone of hysteria making Felice's voice sound the way it used to when, years ago, Luci had violated her curfew and Felice was frantically calling the truant teen's friends for clues to her whereabouts. I wondered if Felice was angry with me because I hadn't told her that Eunice was a stripper.

"Do you have plans for dinner?" I asked. "If not, we could meet at Grimaldi's and talk there. My treat," I added impulsively. I knew business at the bridal shop had fallen off after the terrorist attacks.

"Thanks, Bel. That sounds real good to me," said Felice. She didn't sound angry. "What time?"

"What time do you close today?" I asked.

"Believe it or not, I've got a bridesmaid coming in for a fitting at six, so let's say seven-thirty, just to be safe," Felice answered. "I'll meet you there."

Felice was waiting for me when I arrived. A compact graying woman in a brown Ultrasuede maxi skirt and ecru silk blouse, Felice stood out among the yuppies in sweats and running shoes. She looked tired, her brown eyes circled and her generous mouth contracted into two thin lines now bearing only faint traces of lipstick. We each ordered a beer and agreed to share a pizza topped with fresh mozzerella, fresh basil, tomatoes, and roasted red peppers, a menu miracle that Grimaldi's turned out on a regular basis. "I feel so awful about Eunice," Felice began. "She was probably not much older than our girls."

"I know," I said. "And she was a lovely person, a really hardworking and dedicated teacher, someone who could have made a difference in this lousy world if she'd had half a chance." I reached over and patted my bag on the banquette next to me, reassuring myself that my packet of Kleenex was within reach. Too much reminiscing about Eunice would, I knew, make me cry.

"I didn't know she was a stripper, though. Did you know, Bel?" Felice's question was fair, and her voice was without recrimination.

"Yes, I did. She mentioned it in an essay she wrote for the Faculty Development Seminar I teach. Remember, I told you that's where I met her?" Felice nodded. It was clear that Felice had not contacted me for the purpose of berating me for holding out on her. "I figured she'd have told you eventually. It wasn't really my place to tell you," I said, hearing how disloyal my words might have sounded to someone who, unlike Felice, measured friendship in confidences broken and secrets revealed.

"On your say-so I'd have rented to her anyway," Felice said. "You know that. But I might have given her a talking-to about coming home late and persuaded her to take a cab, like we always told our own girls, remember?" She smiled faintly.

I remembered. "Like they listened," I said returning her faint smile. "It's funny. I thought about saying something like that to her Saturday, but I decided that she wasn't my kid and she was an adult, so I shouldn't play mom. I wonder if she would have listened," I said, feeling guilty all over again.

"Bel, remember how crazy we used to get when the kids were late? Can you imagine if you got a call from a cop telling you Rebecca . . ." There was no need for her to finish the sentence. "Oh God, Bel. Eunice's father called today," Felice said, the arrival of our pizza doing nothing to diminish the hysteria that was unmistakable in her voice now.

"That poor man," I said, remembering that he had not favored his daughter's continuing her education. Nonetheless I empathized with him in his grief. "And her mother too," I said, extricating a Kleenex from my purse.

"I don't know, Bel," Felice said. "I attempted to express my condolences and he cut me off saying something to the effect that he was a farmer and believed that 'as we sow, so shall we reap.' Then he told me that Eunice's body was being shipped back upstate for burial. So I asked him about her things, you know, like when was he coming for them or did she have a friend who would come and go through them and you know what he said, Bel?" I shook my head. "Well, get this. He said he had no intention of risking his life by coming anywhere near New York anytime soon and didn't know of any friends his daughter had. Then he said something about how he and his wife had no use for 'the wages of sin.' I mean, Bel, he was so cold. Finally he told *me* to pack up her things and give them to the Salvation Army. He said I should give her security deposit to the families of the victims of September 11. And that was that."

"Wow. He sounds like a real hard-liner. No wonder Eunice didn't stick around the old homestead. But I'll be glad to help you pack up her things. After all, I got you into this whole mess," I said, realizing at least one reason why Felice had wanted to see me. "And besides, I was Eunice's friend," I added as soon as it occurred to me. "But have the police been through her stuff yet? I'd think they'd want to go through it pretty carefully. After all, it doesn't take a rocket scientist to figure that in her apartment there just might be a clue as to who killed her."

"I figured you were going to ask about that," said Felice. "I had to leave the store and go home today for about an hour while a detective brushed the place for fingerprints and rifled through that poor girl's desk and then surfed her laptop. It was the first time I'd seen her apartment since she moved in." Felice shook her head. "Half her stuff isn't even unpacked yet. It's still in boxes. Anyway, the detective worked very fast. Said he was taking a break from stopping trucks going through the Lincoln Tunnel to search them for bombs," said Felice, shaking her head again, this time at the absurdity that daily life had become.

"I know the local constabulary have been working round the clock," I said, signaling the waitress. "Want to share another beer?"

"Sure," Felice answered. I ordered another Amstel Lite.

"I still feel terrible about getting you involved in this. The last thing you need is more work and more aggravation," I said by way of apology. "Speaking of work and aggravation, how are things going at the shop? Has business picked up at all?"

"Are you kidding? I told you two big fall orders were canceled right away, one because the bride was killed and the other . . . it was the groom." I winced, recalling how Felice had wept telling me this the first time. Now when she continued speaking, her voice was low and her tone one of self-castigation. "Oh, Bel, what was I thinking when I relocated the shop? The rent on the Avenue is about twice what I was paying before. And I took out a small business loan to pay for the renovation. And you know, Ed's magic does not come cheap."

I thought Felice needed a refresher course in pre–September 11 history, which had been obliterated by the shattering events of that day. "You were thinking that the shop would be more visible if it were on the Avenue and that if you moved there you'd increase your already good business. That's what you were thinking. And guess what? You were absolutely 100 percent right. All summer you had more work than you could handle. That shop was Wedding Central. In fact, a month ago you were considering hiring more help, remember?" Without giving her a chance to do more than nod, I ranted on, "So for God's sake, Felice, don't blame yourself for not predicting that terrorists would destroy the World Trade Center and kill thousands of people . . ."

"God, Bel, I love talking to you. Remember when the girls were little and I caught Luci's hand in the car door and we had to take her to the emergency room? She was screaming and screaming and I thought she was going to lose her fingers. Do you remember that?"

"God, yes," I sighed, wishing that I had ordered two beers.

"Do you remember what you told me?" Felice asked, a long-missing sparkle in her eye.

"No," I said.

"You told me that the reason Luci's hand got mangled in the car door was because as a devoted mother, I'd slammed that door extra hard so it would be sure to lock and she wouldn't fall out," Felice reported. "By the time we got to the hospital, you'd actually convinced me that I'd done a good thing. You just better not be moving, Bel."

"I told you, I'm not going anywhere," I said. I was not eager to revisit the subject of Sol's plans versus mine lest my anger at the poor man overflow and turn my chat with Felice into a one-woman gripe session. We had other things to talk about. That's why I asked, "So you're closed on Sunday, right? Do you want to pack up Eunice's things this Sunday?"

"Yes. Sunday's good. The sooner we get the poor kid's apartment emptied, the sooner I can get a new tenant in there. I don't suppose you have anybody else to recommend, do you?"

I ignored Felice's dig and concentrated instead on wiping tomato sauce off my sleeve.

116

CHAPTER 11

Eunice Goodson
Faculty Development Seminar
Revised Introductory Essay
p. 2

. . . I knew if I stayed on the farm like my parents wanted me to, I'd end up like my mother, marrying, having kids, and working hard in the house, the barn, and the fields every day for my whole life. My boyfriend Will was a lot like my dad. He claimed to love me and yet he couldn't see why I wanted to go to college. If I married Will, I'd never get to learn more anatomy and I'd never get to teach except maybe Sunday school.

I planned my escape, applying to the University in secret. They sent my acceptance to my girlfriend's address. I won a scholarship for the first year. The night before freshman orientation, I left the house in the dark, walked to the bus station, and bought a one-way ticket with money I'd saved from baby-sitting. I left a note for my parents saying where I was and not to worry. I left one for Will too. They never forgave me.

By sophomore year, I'd learned to dance, taken out a loan to pay for my first breast enlargement and some costumes, lied about my age, and gotten a job at a nearby roadside club. I took the stage name of La Professora and choreographed a few numbers involving a ruler and a mortarboard. They loved me! I made enough money to repay my loan and send some to my baby sister Andrea so she could join me at the University after she finished high school. She bought a ticket to New York City instead . . .

I didn't read Eunice's revised essay until after Sabbath services that Saturday when I fled the house, which was ringing with hammering and hymns as Ed, who observed a different Sabbath, labored to bring order out of chaos. I couldn't face another minute locked in the bedroom, so I sought refuge in our little backyard garden with its late-blooming impatiens and geraniums. In this urban Eden it was still possible to escape the woes of the world. Sol was due back on Sunday afternoon, and I planned a hearty welcome and a long chat. In the morning, I would help Felice pack up Eunice's belongings and see if I could find anything there that might hint at her killer's identity. Then I would go grocery shopping and surprise my love with a home-cooked meal and, finally, he and I would talk.

In spite of the fact that it was the Sabbath, I carried three sets of student papers into the garden with me. Although I managed to devote Saturday mornings to Sabbath observance, I hadn't yet found a way to put aside an entire day and still get all my work done. And I reasoned that if I didn't have to rush, reading and responding to student writing was like engaging in an extended dialogue with a lot of people, an activity not totally inappropriate to the Sabbath.

I had two sets of speech outlines to go over and one set of drafts from the Faculty Development Seminar. The outlines went fairly quickly. I scribbled comments in the margins: "No, Troy, I don't think wearing a burka will be an effective visual aid for your speech on Afghanistan's women under the Taliban." Or "Elena, Why not read to us something from the Koran as an example?" Or "Point A and Point C appear to be contradictory. What do you think, Tamika?"

The drafts were longer, but I didn't have to respond to them in writing, at least not yet. They were part of the seminar's emphasis on getting faculty from all disciplines to require students to write so that the immense burden of improving their written expression was not borne entirely by the English Department. Called Writing Across the Curriculum, this was a decades-old national movement that still met with resistance from many faculty members. It was my job to teach my less-experienced colleagues how to work with student writers throughout the composing process and to respond effectively to their work without giving up all their free time. I did this by having the members of the seminar brainstorm topics and ideas, free-write, and work with writing partners and groups on peer critiquing, revision, and proofreading.

Sheltered in my private and protected paradise, I felt a chill when I came to Eunice's revision and Nelson's critique. I had forgotten that her work would still be there, among the other papers, like a letter from a ghost. Feeling slightly voyeuristic, I read her paper along with Nelson's suggestions. Like many more experienced writing teachers, he had asked for more details, more examples, and greater elaboration of Eunice's explanation of how and why she became an anatomy prof. Nelson had done a good job responding to her initial draft and encouraging her to expand it. I clipped Eunice's paper and put it on top of the pile so I could access it easily at another time.

Eunice had responded constructively to Nelson's essay too. Her questions had elicited the story of how a visit from a Texas cousin who wanted to see Soprano country had inspired Nelson to write the business plan for a hypothetical tour company as his master's thesis project. And, as Nelson concluded with more than a trace of hubris, "The rest is history." As I sat there holding the paper in my hand, I recalled Nelson and Eunice chatting as they left the seminar. It saddened me to realize that this meant Nelson would need a new writing partner.

By the time I finished going over the last draft and revision, the sun hung low over the rooftops and the air quickly cooled. I headed inside and cached the papers on the dust-covered catch-all table near the phone. I was eager to ransack my collection of clipped recipes in search of one I could prepare in advance and have ready for Sol the next day. Silly me. For a few golden hours, I'd actually forgotten that our kitchen had been reduced to a demolition site. As I scrapped one of my rare impulses to cook, I managed a rueful smile. At a time in our national history when people all over the country were escaping into their kitchens to whip up comfort food, I, alas, was kitchenless. There's nothing like feeling left out of a feeding frenzy to whet the appetite. Suddenly getting something to eat for myself right away became a more pressing priority than planning the next night's dinner. Grabbing a sweater and my purse, I left the house trying to decide which of the many area eateries to honor with my solitary presence.

I don't know if it was the huge bowl of Mongolian barbecue I assembled for myself at the Gobi Grill or the glass of Mango Lassi or the fact that I enjoyed this feast in the grill's simulated yurt beneath a canopy of multicolored silk, but I slept badly. Or maybe it was just estrogen deprivation. Who knows? At any rate, in my feverish dreams a bespectacled Eunice, her body swathed in silk, emerged from a carton of sawdust to swirl in a dervish's dance against the grim backdrop of the ravaged New York skyline. Morning came as a relief. I showered quickly and went to Felice's house ready to work.

Felice led the way into the apartment down four steps from the gate, through the front door, and into darkness in the narrow vestibule. She turned left, groped for a light switch, and the room in front of us blazed into view. My initial thought was that a Buddhist monk would have felt at home there. A row of five neatly labeled cartons lined one wall. The label on the one closest to me read ANDREA. A futon sofa with bedding carefully folded at one end of it was backed up against an adjoining wall.

A small stove, sink, and under-the-counter fridge nestled snugly beneath hanging cabinets along the length of a slightly recessed alcove. I stepped over to the tiny kitchen, noting the teapot, the wok, and the rice steamer on the range top and the simple white mug and bowl in the drain on the counter. Just outside the alcove was a small rectangular kitchen table circa 1945. With a chrome-trimmed gray Formica top and chrome legs, it was undoubtedly a flea-market find. A single red Anjou pear gleamed like an antique gemstone in the center of the tabletop.

Beneath the window that offered a worm's-eye view of the gate, was a computer station and desk flanked by a floor-to-ceiling book-case crammed with hefty-looking anatomy books. On the desk sat a laptop. I knew that if I booted it up, I'd find files for Eunice's classes, including quiz and paper grades and attendance records. Her course outlines and syllabi would be there too. This data would be invaluable to the poor soul recruited to take over teaching Eunice's two classes in the middle of the semester. I took a closer look at the desk. There was a pile of what seemed to be anatomy quizzes topped by a Post-it on which the phrase TO BE GRADED had been neatly printed. Next to this was a neat stack of what appeared to be bills topped by an-other precisely printed Post-it reading TO BE PAID.

"Oh my God! Bel, would you get a load of this!" Felice spoke from across the room where she had opened the closet. Her voice sounded loud in the small, still space. "Geez."

I joined her where she stood at the door of the closet and gaped. This was not the wardrobe of a Buddhist monk. Boas in a rainbow of colors wafted out from hooks on the inside of the door like feathery tentacles. Suspended from hangers were a gold-beaded strapless gown, a long leopard-print skirt with a matching Spandex halter top, a purple minidress with reflective squares on the front, and a pink baby-doll minidress with a high round collar and puffed sleeves. On the floor glittered stiletto heels in leopard, silver, and Lucite along with gold platform sandals with serpentine ankle straps, and a pair of thigh-high white patent-leather boots. In one corner, barely notice-able, were a pair of gray slipper socks and the plain black leather clogs that Eunice had favored for teaching. Above them, neatly folded, hung three pairs of pants, two black and one gray, and a cap and gown, Eunice's academic wardrobe.

"Geez," I echoed when I had recovered enough to speak at all. "I don't know what I had expected to find in her closet, but . . ."

"Yeah. Me either. This stuff is so tacky," said my buddy Felice, the upscale bridal de-signer who wore a simply cut black dress and a string of pearls to all events billed as dressy. No matter how daring the frocks she designed for her young brides, she herself did not display décolletage, saying with a sigh,

"Been there, done that. Don't need to prove I've got cleavage anymore."

"Remember how our girls used to play dress up?" I asked, suddenly picturing Luci and Rebecca tottering around in our discarded high heels, carrying their grandmothers' vintage beaded evening bags, and wearing assorted tutus, veils, tiaras, and other fantasia we'd put together with the help of a nearby thrift shop and Felice's scrap box. "That's what this reminds me of," I added, pointing to the gaudy finery in the closet. "You call it tacky, but it's really just the stuff of make-believe, probably not too different from the bridal fantasies of the white-wedding yuppies you cater to, just in reverse, that's all," I said, pleased with the logic of my new insight.

"Oh Bel, must you intellectualize everything? Just because we liked Eunice and she had to do this kind of work doesn't make the work any less tacky." I'd long ago learned the futility of arguing with Felice once she'd made up her mind, so I let it go. Besides, part of me agreed with her. "Let's see what's in here," Felice said. She pulled open the top drawer of a highboy next to the closet. "Well, we're not talking Victoria's Secret, that's for sure." Felice was right. Eunice's underwear consisted of a few pairs of black tights, white cotton underpants, several rather ordinary bras, one black, one white, and a sturdy sports bra. An overersized navy blue T-shirt had probably served her as a nightgown.

"We're not done looking," I said. My discomfort at looking into the dead woman's lingerie drawer was now running neck and neck with my curiosity about what the well-dressed stripper wore to undress. "Look in here," I insisted, closing the top drawer and opening the one below. I blinked at the sight of rhinestone-studded pasties glittering like jewels in the dark drawer next to a neatly folded Day-Glo fuschia-and-black-striped bikini top. We noted two other brightly colored bikini tops and a tangle of gaudy thongs and garters.

"This stuff is really weird," said Felice, picking up one of the pasties and holding it between her thumb and index finger. I reached into the drawer for another one and was about to pick it up for a closer look when my knuckle brushed against something cold and hard. Carefully plucking away other pasties and thongs like so many pick-up-sticks, I leaned over the drawer.

"Oh my God, Felice," I said, grabbing her arm. "Forget the pasties and check this out. It's handcuffs."

"Geez, Bel. You're right." Felice was still holding the pastie. With her other hand she reached for the cuffs.

"No, don't touch them," I cried, blocking her arm and turning to face her. "The cop missed this, didn't he?" Felice nodded, her face ashen, one outstretched hand frozen over the drawer and the other one trembling so hard that the pastie she still held blinked as it moved in and out of the light.

"Bel, I don't like this. I feel like we're raiding a tomb. I'm so glad you're here with me."

"Right. This would be even harder for either one of us to do alone. Let's check out the bathroom and then try to figure out a plan for storing this stuff," I said, realizing that to Felice I sounded rational and calm. She probably thought I solved a murder every day like a crossword puzzle. "I'd think better if I had a bagel or something, wouldn't you?"

Leading the way, Felice said, "Probably. But what do you mean 'storing' this stuff? I thought we were giving it to the Salvation Army or Goodwill."

"We are, but some of it needs to be stored temporarily," I said, following Felice into the tiny square enclosure where an enterprising plumber had managed to squeeze a stall shower, sink, and toilet. Felice stepped into the shower to make room for me. The monastic theme prevailed here too. The shower curtain was an opaque no-nonsense white as were the two towels hanging in square folds from dowels.

But the Zen aura did not extend to the contents of the medicine chest. When I opened its mirrored door, we beheld a dazzling rainbow of nail enamels from turquoise to burgundy, vials full of nail glitter, and even one large bottle labeled BODY GLITTER. False eyelashes in several colors occupied a shelf next to a jar of wig shampoo. A fat tube of cocoa butter stood upright in a glass with several slim tubes. There was a small basket full of lipsticks and other makeup and another holding razors, toothpaste, deodorant, moisturizer, dental floss, and other personal hygiene necessities.

"So what's this about storing Eunice's stuff? I don't like the sound of that. I thought we could just box it or bag it and take it all to the Salvation Army." Felice spoke between bites of a lightly buttered bagel and sips of coffee that we had brought back from the *bodega* on the corner. Her color had returned, but since we had found the handcuffs, she was more eager than ever to empty her apartment of Eunice's tainted belongings.

"Too easy. Since when do we do things the easy way?" I said. "Here's what I think." I inhaled deeply, as if to fortify myself for objections. "Her books should be boxed and donated to the RECC library. I'll load them into the trunk of my car and drive them over myself. I'm sure they can use an infusion of anatomy texts. The library won't accept books that are underlined, but I can put those out in the lounge and students will take them. Do you have any idea what text-books cost these days?" Felice was nodding, so I knew that so far she was buying into my plan. "Then there's that laptop," I continued. "I'd like to go through her files and put her grades, her syllabi, her attendance records, and all that stuff on a floppy disk and give it to whoever takes over her class."

"And, of course, you just might peek at her e-mail and her other files while you're at it," said Felice arching one eyebrow. "Bel, I don't want to get involved in any sleuthing. Besides, the detective did cruise through her laptop. He copied some of the stuff, but if you ask me, he seemed much more interested in her wardrobe than in her grade book. Frankly, I just want to empty the apartment so I can get another tenant in and get a rent roll going again."

"I know. But you're right, I probably won't be able to resist going over her e-mail." I shook my head, unable to deny my own nosiness. "But don't worry, I'll work fast." This assurance seemed to satisfy Felice. "And you know what? I bet one or two of Eunice's colleagues at the strip club would like her work clothes and shoes. I mean if there's somebody who wears her size . . ."

Felice nodded, and spoke like the seasoned retailer she was. "You're right. Even though that stuff looks cheap, it's probably not. And what about the laptop? I suppose somebody could really use that too. It looks fairly new." I was glad to hear Felice agreeing to dispose of Eunice's pathetic legacy in a way that honored the dead woman rather than following her father's dismissive dictum.

"You're so right," I said, thinking of the many RECC students still living on the other side of the digital divide without a computer at home. "Let's think about that. Now what about the boxes along the wall? We don't even know what's in them, do we?"

"No. But we can find out," said Felice standing up and resting her hands on her hips. I could tell she was eager for us to stop chatting and do something. "Listen, I brought some boxes in from the store and I can always run over and get more. Let's get the books packed and loaded into your car. Then we can pack up the clothes and the dishes and put them and the unpacked boxes into my shed. I mean why not? That way we can go through them at our leisure and I can start showing this place empty except for furniture tomorrow. I can call the Salvation Army and ask them to pick that up, right?"

Enormously pleased that Felice had volunteered her shed without my asking, I stood and said, "Sure. Sounds like a plan." We turned and once more headed downstairs into the basement apartment.

CHAPTER 12

Woodstock. Quaint 2 br seasonal bungalow with year-round potential. Wbf and screened-in porch. Sloping, partially wooded 3-acre lot with mountain views. New septic system. 10 miles to town. $250,000.

"But Bel, you should see it. You'd love it. It's on three acres. Five months a year you could do yoga outdoors. You could have a real garden, not just an overgrown patio with a border of annuals like you have here. And there's a view of the mountains. We could hike every day like we do in Maine. And the town is only twenty minutes away. You drive past rolling hills and barns. You should see the foliage now . . ." Sol's voice had risen with the urgency of his desire to share his bucolic vision.

"But Sol, we have a real garden. It takes a morning to plant the entire border with colorful blossoms every spring and this seasonal exertion completely satisfies my extremely limited urge to till the soil." Even as I could hear my own voice rising, I could see that Sol was oblivious to my sarcasm, but still I continued. "I am perfectly happy doing yoga inside on my yoga mat where my allergies don't act up. When I want to see mountains, I look at a landscape painting or drive to the country. But frankly, I'd rather look at neighbors and shop windows and kids playing and . . ." Frustrated that I had let him manipulate me into arguing over the trees when he was missing the forest, I threw up my hands. Sol had walked into the house waving realtors brochures and ranting about acres and mountains. But instead of refocusing the conversation onto his post-traumatic stress syndrome and what we could do about it, I was actually honoring his nutty schemes with logical responses. Whatever had happened to my intention to hear him out, to talk this through civilly?

My good intentions had become casualties of sadness and fatigue. Sorting Eunice's books and packing and lugging boxes of the dead woman's things all day had taken its toll. What's more, I missed the man who used to comfort and cajole me. He was gone again, replaced by this raving apologist for pastoral pleasures who seemed like a total stranger. This impression was further corroborated when Sol said, "And the house, Bel, I tell you, you've got to see it. It's perfect for us. It needs a little work, winterizing and maybe a new roof, but . . ."

I lost it. We were strolling en route to an as

132

yet undetermined restaurant when I stopped, turned to face Sol and began speaking slowly and emphatically in a tone just a little too loud to pass as conversational. "Sol, our own house is perfect for us. We're spending our last dime making it that way. Finally we're going to have floor-through air-conditioning, replacement windows, and a super kitchen with all new appliances. That's why we're enduring this hellish renovation. And if you think I'm ever going to go through another one in my lifetime . . ." I jerked my elbow away from his hand as, aware of the stares of bypassers, he attempted to turn me around and propel me forward once again.

We resumed walking but continued on in silence for nearly a block as we headed automatically to the river. For a moment I thought that might have been a mistake. Smoke still emanated from the smoldering buildings across the Hudson. The skyline now looked unfinished, like the silhouette of a face without a chin. And the wrought-iron fence separating the walkway from the river below had become a shrine hung with photos, poetry, and flowers. We stared at the faces of the dead, who stared back at us through sightless eyes.

Maybe it was an optical illusion caused by the ebbing daylight and my mounting sorrow, but for a moment I thought the face in the photo nearest me was Eunice's. Just as my throat tightened and my eyes filled, Sol grabbed my arm again, this time to give and get comfort. We stood there, arm in arm, trying once more to take in the enormity of the loss of life and innocence. I was about to tell him about my vision when he spoke. "It could happen again, Bel. That's what gets me. That's why I want us to move. Lots of people are leaving this area. We were lucky this time. Let's not press our luck. We could manage a move."

I saw the smoke through my own tears, now falling freely. I heard Sol's words over the pounding of my heart. I resolved to use my not inconsiderable powers of persuasion to convince Sol that we'd be okay in Hoboken, to get him to talk to a shrink. After all, how many of my own midlife crises had this man talked me through? I smiled, recalling the river walk we'd taken the day my daughter had e-mailed me jarring news of her impending shotgun wedding. Sol had offered compassion and comfort that morning, even as he refuted my lapses of logic. I shook my head remembering that same sunny day when we had found the bloody body of a local Frank Sinatra impersonator not five hundred yards from where we were standing. In retrospect the events of that afternoon ran through my mind like black-and-white photos from an old family album, snapshots taken in a long-ago and far-simpler time.

What I said was, "We can talk more over dinner. I've had kind of a rough couple of days and you must be tired too." Sol's baby-sitting stints always left him both exhilarated and exhausted. "Where should we eat?" I asked, as gently as I could.

"Italian, Thai, or Cuban?" Sol said, leaving the decision to me. For once I didn't care what sort of cuisine we had as long as we ate in a quiet place, one where we could sit and talk without interruption for as long as it took.

"Actually I'm in the mood for a booth at Helmer's," I said, naming an old uptown Hofbrau house left over from the days when many German immigrants had settled in Hoboken. Helmer's still served sauerbraten and dumplings. And each of the scarred high-backed wooden booths lining the walls of the old barroom was a cozy dark nook promising privacy.

"Sure. We haven't been there in years," said Sol. "I guess our cholesterol count is kind of irrelevant now," he added with a touch of black humor. Still arm in arm, we ambled uptown, enjoying the night air. The booth at Helmer's did not disappoint, and we settled in and ordered. Even before our beer came, I struggled to listen and reserve judgment as Sol resumed his sales pitch. "Bel, what have you got against living in a less densely populated area? You should see Cold

Springs. It's a charming little village, just like the towns you always want to stop in when we go to Maine. You'd love the antique shops, and there's an eatery serving home-made soup and country cooking . . ."

"Sol, I don't want to move. And I don't think you really want to move either," I said softly, watching his eyes register surprise at where I wanted to focus the conversation. But it was time for us to stop talking real estate and say more about what was really on our minds. "No, I think you're suffering from post-traumatic stress, and you need to talk to someone about it." The waitress arrived and placed steins of Lindeman's framboise on the table.

"Are you serious?" Sol said. "*You* want *me* to see a shrink?" He looked at me as if I'd just suggested that he promenade naked down the Avenue.

Ignoring the implication inherent in his projected pronouns, I said, "Yes, love. I do. Since you witnessed the destruction of the World Trade Center, you've been worried about another attack on this area and suggesting that we move to the country. To me that seems like an extreme response." Again I spoke quietly, the way I spoke to students who feared giving their first public speech or attending their first job interview. He shrugged, not denying the truth of what I said. I took that as an invitation to continue.

"You've always been the one who kept my impulsive behavior in check. You've always included me in decision making. Also, Sol, we both know you love urban living and you love Hoboken."

"And I love you." He reached across the table and grabbed my hand. "Bel, let's get married. Will you marry me?" Now it was my turn to register surprise. Damn. The man was impossible. For years he'd been proposing regularly on the anniversary of our first meeting even though he knew I had no intention of ever doing the marriage thing again. But this proposal was different. "Hear me out," Sol was saying. "If you retire early, you'll lose your health benefits." My surprise grew closer to utter amazement with each word that came out of his mouth. "But if we're married, I can put you on my retirement plan for only a small monthly premium. And it's a good plan, Bel." I didn't know whether to laugh or cry.

Trying not to betray my astonishment at the sheer *chutzpah* of his proposition, I took a deep breath and, in a moment of inspiration, got ready to offer what I hoped was a no-lose counterproposal. "How romantic, Sol," I said, looking into his eyes for even a trace of his familiar deviltry. "Tell you what. I'll make a deal with you."

His eyes held mine. "What's the deal?" he asked, playing with the fingers of my hand.

"See a shrink for at least ten sessions and I'll marry you." There it was, out on the table, the best I could offer. Would he take it?

I knew I had won this round when his face broke out in the grin I remembered, and he said, "Deal." Raising our steins, we sealed our bargain with a toast. By the time my sauerbraten and Sol's steak sandwich came, we were engaged.

CHAPTER 13

To: Andybgood@hotmail.com
From: Egoodson@hotmail.com
Re: Your gear
Date: 09/08/01 19:39:32

Andrea,

Sorry about changing the lock, but did you really expect me to let you stay on after you took my tips from all of last week, my CD player, and the bracelet Will gave me? If you did, then that poison has really gotten to you. I've packed your things and moved them with me to my new apartment. If you e-mail me where to ship them, I'll send them to you. I'm changing this e-mail address in a few weeks, so you better get back to me pronto.

Eunice

"That e-mail from Eunice to Andrea was the only item in Eunice's computer that offered a lead," I explained, pointing to the copy on the table where Illuminada, Betty, and I had gathered over lunch.

"So who do you think Andrea is?" asked Betty between spoonfuls of chicken noodle soup. We were at the RIP Diner, a humble all-purpose eatery close to RECC where for lack of a college cafeteria, students, staff, and faculty routinely gathered to gorge and gossip.

"She must be her sister. Eunice mentioned a baby sister named Andrea in here," I said, pointing to Eunice's essay that I had copied and given to Illuminada and Betty. "And at least one box in her apartment is labeled 'Andrea.' "

"Right," said Illuminada. "The poor woman got ripped off by her druggie sister and kicked her out, and then, *dios mío*," Illuminada shrugged at what she saw as a familiar chain of events. She cut off a tiny corner of her tuna melt and popped it into her mouth.

Betty was eager to fill in her version of the back-story. "So you're saying this Andrea is the younger sister who couldn't hack life down on the farm anymore either and got strung out in the big city?"

Illuminada nodded before asking, "Bel, how did you figure out Eunice's e-mail address or did you get Sol to do it?" Illuminada was quite proud of her own hacking prowess.

"Well, actually, I did get Sol to do it. He has a lot of trouble sleeping lately, so he gets through the night playing computer solitaire.

140

I asked him if instead of playing games on the computer in the wee hours, he would figure out how to access Eunice's RECC files and put them on a disk. Then I suggested that he also go through her e-mail for anything that might throw light on her death. I told him it would help his buddy Charlie. But Sol didn't really need persuading." As I spoke, I recalled the set of Sol's jaw when he had agreed to crack the code that would, perhaps, give him access to the dead woman's killer. "You know . . ." I paused, unable to resist contemplating Sol's worrisome state of mind.

"Do we know what, *chiquita?*" asked Illuminada, daintily impaling another bite of tuna melt on her fork. "Finish your sentence before you drift off, please."

"You know, Sol still thinks we're going to get married and move to a cabin in the boonies where boredom is the biggest killer. He figures all our problems will end when our covered wagon reaches the city limits," I said, polishing off the last juicy bite of a rare cheeseburger.

"So should we be planning a bridal shower?" asked Betty, only half facetiously. Then she looked me straight in the eye and said, "Girlfriend, you make fun of Sol's ideas, but, you know, lots of folks *are* moving. And you wouldn't be the first person to retire early either."

I stared at my good friend, aghast at what

I took to be the idiocy of her comment. "Hel-lo, Betty. Didn't I just get my Ph.D.? I'm a more effective teacher than I ever was. And I'm finally leading the Faculty Development Seminar like I've always wanted to. I'm at the top of my game. It doesn't get any better. Why on earth would I want to leave my work, leave my students?"

"Well, *chiquita*, I hate to break it to you, but soon you'll be pushing the big Six-O. And if you and Sol can afford it, you just might want to stop working so hard and, as they say, smell the roses . . ." said Illuminada, answering for Betty, who for once in her life looked a bit taken aback by the vehemence of my response.

"I've smelled the roses in the country, and they smell boring," I said, pushing my plate away as if with that gesture I could also dismiss the whole notion of retiring and moving, which for some reason my closest friends suddenly seemed to be championing. "And who knows what anybody can afford in these crazy times? Hey, are you two trying to get rid of me?" I asked. I hoped my voice didn't betray the irritation I felt.

"No, but we will be if we have to stop figuring out who killed Eunice to do your retirement planning," said Betty. "Remember, President Woodman himself charged you with solving this one. And of course the Illysario girl's parents are also counting on you. So before you roll over your 403(b) to an IRA . . ."

I was so surprised to find Illuminada's customary role as timekeeper usurped by Betty that I was momentarily quiet. "Point well taken," I finally said as graciously as I could. "I do have a plan." Illuminada cocked her head in anticipation, and Betty got out her Palm Pilot.

"How would you like to spend an evening or two in Manhattan at the Big Apple Peel?" I asked, expecting my idea to be shot down by my rather straight-laced friends. "I'm sure that's where we'll find leads to Eunice's killer."

"I'm not so sure. What about her sister? She sounds like an obvious suspect to me," said Illuminada. "*La familia*. Remember to always check out the family first." Illuminada's work experience had taught her that most assailants and their victims were related. My life experience had taught me that relatives like to keep you around to make you crazy.

"What about the guy Eunice dumped when she went to college?" said Betty, her fingers flying over her tiny Palm Pilot. "Maybe he still cares and came up here to win her back and . . ."

I was trying to imagine my high school boyfriend, carrying a torch for six years and then following me to New York to win me back. That would have seriously interfered with David Einhardt's rebound romance with the buxom and reportedly compliant Susie Teitelbaum not to mention his progress in dental school. Illuminada's voice interrupted me just as I flashed on the image of David and Susie slow dancing at the prom. "Well, that's a reach, but her sister . . . Illuminada, why don't you find out from one of your buddies at County Homicide if they've checked out Andrea Goodson?" I asked. There wasn't a local agency including the police departments and County Homicide that didn't have at least one grateful former client of Illuminada's on the payroll. "She's such an obvious suspect that I can't believe somebody hasn't brought her in for questioning."

"*Sí, chiquita,*" said Illuminada. "There's no reason why we have to reinvent the wheel. But there's no mention of her here." She pushed across the table toward me a sheaf of papers that I recognized as a police report. "The most interesting thing in here is the medical examiner's assertion that the chest wound was a puncture, not a slash," said Illuminada.

"Thanks," I said, smoothing the front page of the document before stashing it in my book bag. I didn't want to dwell on the details of Eunice's death. "In the meantime, are you game to go to the Big Apple Peel with me?"

"But we'll stand out there like chaperones at a prom," said Illuminada. "I bet Raoul,

Sol, and Vic could go though."

"No. We're going ourselves. I've got it all figured out," I snapped. "Betty, can we meet at the funeral parlor with Vic late tomorrow afternoon, after we all get out of work?"

"Sure," said Betty with a slight shrug. "Whatever you say, Bel."

That little lift of her shoulders and her docile response belied her discomfort. Betty always chafed when she was in a show that someone else was running. I confess that my already self-satisfied smile widened at the thought of making my favorite control freak squirm just a little.

CHAPTER 14

To: Bbarrett@circle.com
From: Mnewton@piccadilly.co.uk
Re: Renovation blues
Date: 10/30/01 10:13:44

Dear Down and Dirty in Hoboken,

Saw your posting on the renovation support group bulletin board. I sympathize with your impatience and frustration, but at least your contractor is doing a decent, if somewhat extended and messy, job. Perchance our story will provide you some perspective and make you feel a bit easier. We've just terminated our contractor. The silly bloke was supposed to install a concrete floor and drainage system in what is to be our new plant conservatory. The bloody yahoo put the drain at the top of the slight incline instead of the bottom, and since water doesn't flow uphill, even I can see that the damn thing will never work properly. How did we respond to this? I'm sitting at our local pub e-mailing you and having a pint while across the table from me my husband is having his third pint of the morning and telephoning our solicitor. I hope you have a pub nearby. And a solicitor.

Cheers,
Madge

I didn't have time to drink myself through the rest of the renovation. I had classes to teach, papers to respond to, the rest of Eunice's things to sort through and give away, and her killer to nail. And then there was Sol. He was still sleeping poorly. And since 9/11 whenever a helicopter roared over our house on a routine check of commuter traffic, he flinched. I was afraid he was about to start circling real estate ads again. And he didn't have another appointment with his therapist for ten days. Fortunately, Sol was chairing a meeting of the Citizens Committee to Preserve the Waterfront that night, so he wouldn't mind that I was going out.

I drove to Vallone and Sons Funeral Home, owned and operated by Vic Vallone since the deaths of his dad and brother. As a funeral director, Vic could be counted on to have lots of clothing, accessories, props, and makeup on hand because many of his clients expected their deceased relatives to dress to the nines in death. Betty referred rather irreverently to this collection of get-ups as "the costume shop." It had come in handy during other investigations when we

147

had found it necessary to disguise ourselves.

Betty and Illuminada had already arrived. They were chatting in an anteroom waiting for me and for Vic, who was meeting with a client in his office. I'd attended at least three wakes in that room, but that afternoon with the light from the setting sun streaming in the stained-glass window and my two friends gabbing, the place was almost cheerful. "Bel, just tell me we don't have to do any exotic dancing," said Betty. "I'm a little out of shape for that, and Vic doesn't have G-strings or pasties in the costume shop."

"Me too, *chiquita*," said Illuminada grinding her slim hips a couple of times before she sank into a chair. "I hope that's not why you dragged us over to this house of death. There's no way . . ."

"No, we're not going to be dancing. We're going to be in the audience in drag." I announced.

"You've got to be kidding, Bel," said Betty. "We may not look like club girls, but we sure as hell don't look like guys either."

"*Dios mío*, Bel. What are you going to do with those?" Illuminada chuckled as she pointed at my not exactly masculine-looking chest.

"It's very simple, right, Vic?" Vic was entering the room as I spoke. He paused to embrace Betty for what seemed like an hour.

Illuminada and I glanced at each other, shrugged, and rolled our eyes. Betty and Vic's romance was one of the best things that had ever happened to either of them. In defiance of reason, custom, and culture, and amid the detritus of death and divorce, their love had taken root and grown. We teased them about it whenever there was an opening. "As I was about to say before we were treated to this X-rated display, Vic will outfit us in suits, beards, wigs, hats, and whatever else it takes to make us look credible as guys. Then we go to the Big Apple Peel and watch and listen and see what we can learn."

As soon as he had disentangled himself from Betty, Vic smiled. He said, "I'll see what I've got. Give me a minute." Then he disappeared, heading for the room where he stored the makings of masquerade. By the time we boarded separate cars of the PATH train for New York an hour later, Betty, Illuminada, and I were completely transformed. I wore a long black beard that Vic had trimmed until it was scraggly and a wig of unkempt shoulder-length black hair. Vic had found me a dark, preworn men's suit and a white dress shirt under which I had on a sports bra I'd outgrown years before. To complete my metamorphosis, Vic handed me a scuffed violin case. "This belonged to a musician who wanted to be viewed and buried with his violin, so I hung on to the case," Vic said. "You look just like an out-of-work pit violinist not too long off the boat." He stepped back a few feet to admire his handiwork.

"*Spasibo*," I said, thanking him for the compliment in my new language. If I had to speak at all, I'd decided to adapt a thick Russian accent in the hope that, along with the loud music that would undoubtedly accompany the dancers, it would distract listeners from my voice. My accent owed more to Yiddish than Russian, but only a purist would notice. Years ago over blini in the old Russian Tea Room, Sol had taught me how to say *please* and *thank you* in Russian.

Meanwhile Illuminada had morphed into a bearded and bespectacled young lackey. A backwards baseball cap hid most of her hair, and her slight frame was bowed down under my backpack. She wore baggy jeans and a baggy shirt and pushed a wheelchair in which Betty had ensconced herself. Now bearded, suited, fedora-ed, and padded to plumpness, Betty sat with one leg extended in a fake cast Vic had improvised. She looked like Al Sharpton with a broken leg. We had agreed that Illuminada would speak Spanish and Betty would keep quiet.

According to the plan we had fleshed out while Vic was concocting our disguises, we exited the PATH train in Manhattan at fourteenth Street and Sixth Avenue. While Illuminada and Betty looked for a working elevator to bring them to street level, I headed straight for the Big Apple Peel. My research had located it a few blocks away in an area just south of artsy Chelsea and east of the newly trendy meatpacking district, but without the cachet of either. The neighborhood's total lack of distinction was probably what had saved the Big Apple Peel from Mayor Giuliani's cleanup crusade. Unlike Times Square, this area would not attract major corporate developers anytime soon. It was a hodgepodge of Caribbean delis and nontrendy Asian restaurants. I noted a seedy-looking photography studio over a now defunct karate school, a few rundown apartments, and the windowless back wall of a warehouse that fronted on Fifteenth Street.

In fact, the Big Apple Peel, with its newly sand-blasted and repointed brick façade and elegant wrought-iron trimmed marquee, was the classiest building on the block. A representation of a partially peeled apple in red and green neon and the words

EXOTIC DANCING! STRIP TEASE!
FEATURING SALOMÉ

Printed in black on a white background flashed discreetly from the marquee. Beneath it hung a large American flag.

As I approached the club, the absurdity of what I was about to do hit me. What was a nice Jewish fifty-something English prof doing entering a strip club at 8 p.m. on a Tuesday night? Or at any time, for that matter? And in drag? I should be home reading student papers or at RECC teaching an evening class. Or, if I got lucky, I might be a few blocks uptown waiting for the curtain to rise on a Broadway play. Instead, I was a costumed actor in an unlikely drama of my own design, a burlesque. What was I thinking? I didn't even approve of stripping. Maybe it paid the bills, but didn't it also objectify women and so encourage violence against us? Before I could spook myself with further reflections on the absurdity, not to mention the political incorrectness, of what I was doing, I entered the Big Apple Peel.

CHAPTER 15

Http://www.thebigapplepeel.com/homepage
The Big Apple Peel
515 West Fourteenth Street
New York, New York 10004
212-413-4488
Don't miss New York's
hottest tourist destination!

Enjoy *"Manhattan Madness,"* a chorus line of the Big Apple Peel's sexiest girls who give new meaning to a medley of musical tributes to the Big Apple. Kick back, sip a drink, and marvel at our fabulous featured dancers. Later at Big Apple Academy, the Big Apple Spa, Fifth Avenue, or the Big Apple Art Museum, you can watch your favorite New York fantasies made flesh. Cover charge and hours. Group arrangements.

The night before, I'd visited the Big Apple Peel's website. Clicking on COVER CHARGE AND HOURS had prepared me for the fifty dollars we had to fork over to the green-gowned greeter smiling at me above her cleavage and her cash register. She was strategically located behind a glass display case stocked with souvenirs of Manhattan. There were T-shirts, sweat shirts, ashtrays, mugs, paperweights, postcards, and photos all emblazoned with I LOVE NY and the apple logo. I recalled Mayor Giuliani's edict that sex businesses in New York had to devote at least 40 percent of their floor space to non-sex-related objects. For the Big Apple Peel, compliance was a gratuitous exercise in self-promotion.

But nothing I'd clicked on had prepared me for the sight of eight nearly naked women gyrating to the familiar strains of "New York, New York" amplified to a deafening roar. I reminded myself that I was a horny Russian green-card holder alone in the Big Apple. I gaped at the dancers. On a stage that snaked out among the tables scattered around the large room, the women moved with the beat, grinding their hips and thrusting forward the tiny white sequined triangles winking at the front of their G-strings. In unison they reached behind them, unsnapped their red-and-blue bikini tops, and flipped them aside. I took a seat at an unoccupied table and ordered a "Smirnoff on rocks, pliz," from a scantily clad waitress. When I looked up, I was astonished to see a row of bright red-and-blue nipples bobbing across the stage. *Were they painted? Dyed? Was it the lighting? Whatever the process, was it harmful? Permanent?*

I didn't have a chance to work through the

answers to these questions. The hairs on the back of my neck tingled when in the audience of Asian men in suits, American men in suits, older men in sports coats and slacks, and a few younger men in jeans or chinos, I spotted a familiar face. One of the younger men was Jorge Malagas, a decidedly lackluster student who had been in my Intro to Lit class the past semester. What was he doing here? One look at his face answered this prize-winning question. Jorge's eyes rotated with the dancers' twirling tassels while at regular intervals his tongue flicked over his parted lips. He had not been half this attentive in Intro to Lit. The more pressing question was what if he recognized me. Assuming I was safe until the dancers left the stage, I resolved to look for Jorge's name on Eunice's rosters. What he was doing there seemed obvious, but I wanted to check him out anyway.

In the meantime, I tried to remain in character and focus on the dancers. Every now and then, one of them would stop gyrating in the line and kneel or bend down and writhe for the personal pleasure of whomever happened to be nearest at that moment. The individual so favored would wedge a bill somewhere on the dancer's person, between her breasts, under her G-string or, in one case, between the cheeks of her butt. Before I could do more than fumble in my pocket for a five-dollar bill, I was eyeball to blue

155

nipple with an undulating dancer. She was so close, I could see the pores on her skin and smell the faint musky odor of her perfumed sweat. Awkwardly I placed the five with several others under her G-string and muttered *"spasibo."* Imagine my reaction when, grinning broadly, she whispered, *"Nye za shto"* before she stood and joined the others for the finale, a patriotic pyramid of boobs and crotches. The Cold War was definitely over.

Just then I noticed a wiry little white guy pushing a portly black man in a wheel chair through the door. At the same time, the dancers returned and joined the waitresses circulating among the tables hawking overpriced drinks, snacks, and souvenirs. I watched Illuminada stand and push Betty through the door labeled FIFTH AVENUE. Steeling myself, I decided to venture into BIG APPLE ACADEMY, one of the other "specialty rooms" that had been advertised on the club's website, but it was nowhere to be seen.

I finished my drink and made my way through the door labeled BIG APPLE ART MUSEUM instead. I found myself standing with a cluster of about ten other spectators in front of a Lucite screen that separated us from a small stage. An elaborate gilded frame rose from the front end of the stage where three costumed dancers were taking turns posing as the subjects of famous paintings.

156

The man next to me slipped a five through a slot in the Lucite screen. Transfixed, I watched as the Mona Lisa slowly removed her signature black gown to the strains of "A Certain Smile." Additional fives pushed through the slot assured the progression of her strip. By the time she was down to her G-string, the music had shifted to the "Waltz of the Flowers" and a ballerina in a gauzy pale pink tutu entered *en pointe*. The lovely dancer bent to adjust her toe shoe strap, mirroring the pose of one of Degas's dancers. It wasn't long before, also encouraged by the flyers her fans fed through the slot, she too had stripped to her G-string. Finally, an artfully draped blue-and-ecru head wrap and a golden frock turned a young stripper into the girl with the pearl earring immortalized by Vermeer. She gracefully removed her costume at five-dollar intervals. I thought the performance was over. But then each of the dancers slowly dressed and assumed her original pose, further titillating her slack-jawed viewers.

I turned to leave when suddenly my heart flipped over and stopped beating. Between me and the door stood Nelson Vandergast. What if *he* recognized me? He was less than a foot away and I had to walk literally under his nose to get out of the room. Willing myself to move forward, I sidled along behind the knot of men closest to the Lucite screen and in front of Nelson, my head averted. But, again, I needn't have worried. Like every other man there, Nelson was still ogling the tableau of dancers framed in gilt. Without seeing me, he moved aside so I could get by him. I closed the door behind me and exhaled with relief.

I glanced at my watch. It was only 9:30, but I felt as if I had been there forever, trapped in a strange and noisy world where familiar female body parts seemed alien and aliens became familiars. Betty, Illuminada, and I had agreed to meet back at the funeral home around ten, and I was eager to be out of there before I ran into anybody else who might blow my cover. As I walked through the bar, I noticed that the line of dancers had been replaced by a tall, red-haired soloist draped in a diaphanous gown of gold and silver, the featured Salomé, no doubt. I didn't stick around to see her dance out of her veils or behead the hapless prophet. I'd had enough tabloid tableaux for one night.

I walked the few blocks back to the PATH train, enjoying the relative peace and quiet of the busy thoroughfare. The proclivity of many young people to live their lives accompanied by overamplified screams and percussive banging had long mystified me. The crowd at the Big Apple Peel was not an especially young one, but all the music had been eardrum shattering nonetheless, even in the Big

Apple Art Museum. It was hard to picture the contemplative and soft-spoken Eunice Goodson spending hours a day amid such bedlam. It was also hard to imagine her with red or blue nipples. How did they do that?

I did not solve this preoccupying riddle let alone figure out who had killed Eunice on my way back to Vallone and Sons. Vic had been working late in the office and was waiting for us. It was comforting to see a man who was not slack-jawed. Before too long, Betty and Illuminada returned, and we retired to the anteroom to change. We were too tired to talk much. "Can I buy you gals a drink?" asked Vic as soon as we emerged dressed as ourselves. "I'm about to close up here." He looked tired too. His eyes were ringed with dark smudges and his shoulders slumped.

"No thanks, Vic, I had to down a vodka on the rocks and I'm sure I'll feel that tomorrow. I haven't had the hard stuff in decades," I said. "But I couldn't exactly order a glass of house Merlot, could I?"

"How about a milk shake then? Or a malted? I really don't want to miss the replay on this one. Come on," said Vic, not about to take no for an answer. "As a favor to your costume designer."

In a few minutes we four were seated at the RIP, never distinguished for its food, but renowned for scrumptious back-to-the-fifties

sodas, malts, and shakes. I ordered a chocolate malted. "Come to think of it, I haven't
had one of these in decades either," I said.
Betty and Vic ordered coffee shakes, and
Illuminada ordered a vanilla float. "You
know, it's nice to be having something that
doesn't have the word *latte* in the title or *ino*
at the end for a change, isn't it?"

"Listen, *chiquita*, it's just nice to be sitting
down after pushing this Al Sharpton look-
alike around for two hours," said Illuminada,
gesturing in Betty's direction.

"Easy there, you're talking about the
woman I love," said Vic, throwing his arm
around Betty. He looked a little livelier now
that we were out of the funeral home and
about to ingest some serious sugar. "So tell
all. What did you make of the Big Apple
Peel?"

"How do they get their nipples red and
blue?" I blurted, aware as I spoke that this
was not, perhaps, salient to our investigation
of Eunice's death. Vic looked quizzical.

"See, there are flags everywhere and they
wore red-white-and-blue costumes, so when
they stripped . . ." Betty didn't finish her explanation. Our drinks came, and we all
paused to take that first slurp, the slurp that
recalled to me every chocolate malted I'd
ever consumed as a teenager. I closed my
eyes to savor the memories and the rich
flavor of the malt. "Bel, don't drift into a

160

chocolate-induced stupor," Betty said. She reached across the table and snapped her fingers in my face. It's a good thing Proust didn't share snacks with Betty, or he'd never have written a word.

"Yes, *chiquita*. Tomorrow is a workday. Let's get on with it." Illuminada was back in her usual role as clock-watcher. "Did you see anything or anyone worth a second visit?"

"The cover charge is pretty steep, but we knew that from the website," I said. I was thinking out loud rather than answering Illuminada's question. "Would you believe I saw a RECC colleague there? He's taking my Faculty Development Seminar, for God's sake! And a former student! They didn't recognize me in drag," I added, punchy now from fatigue and sensory overload. Soon the sugar would kick in. I was counting on it. "I was surprised to see a RECC prof or student coughing up fifty bucks for a strip club."

Vic, who looked a little disappointed at the desultory conversation he'd had such hopes for, said, "Why not? No law says RECC profs and students don't appreciate naked women. Besides, that club's got a great location, near the PATH and several Manhattan subway lines. A lot of other guys from New Jersey probably go there, especially commuters."

"I guess so," I said. "The prof I saw was Eunice's writing partner in the Faculty Devel-

161

opment Seminar." In unison Betty and Illuminada looked up over their straws, suddenly attentive. "His name's Nelson Vandergast, the business adjunct who has a day job leading tours of Soprano sites. I'm sure I told you about him." Together they shook their heads. "He wrote a eulogy for Eunice that he wants to read aloud. It was very decent of him." My voice trailed off as I began to synthesize the implications of Nelson's presence there among the glazed-eyed gawkers. What had gone on between the two writing partners? "I'll have to check him out too. He and Eunice might have seen each other outside the seminar . . ."

"He sounds like a viable suspect to me, definitely worth checking out. He knew the victim and, who knows, he might have had a thing about her," said Illuminada.

"So you came up with something in that tourist trap of a strip joint, after all," said Vic, shaking his head. Although he was always willing to help us, it was no secret that Vic often considered our investigative technique just this side of cockamamie.

"I can't picture Eunice Goodson in that environment. It was so loud, so . . ." I hesitated. "They have these specialty rooms listed on the web." Vic looked puzzled again. "They're just rooms where you can see your fantasies enacted. That is if you have these types of fantasies," I said, trying to imagine a man who would entertain sexual fantasies about the Mona Lisa. "I went into the one called the Big Apple Art Museum. The stage was in a gold picture frame and the dancers were costumed as women in famous paintings, like the Mona Lisa. And she really looked like the Mona Lisa too. Anyway, there was a slot in a Lucite screen for money. Every time somebody put in a five, the dancer took off another layer. After she was practically naked, she very slowly got dressed again."

"The Mona Lisa doesn't do it for me," said Vic. "What other art did they have? Anything by Picasso? Modigliani? Any impressionist pieces?"

Before Betty could elbow the grin off his face, Illuminada said, "We went into the Big Apple Spa room. This must be the destination for the guys like you whose fantasies probably run more toward muscles and soapsuds. First they had this gal in Spandex workout clothes doing gymnastic tricks with a floor-to-ceiling pole. Then she lifted dumbbells. After she did a few reps, guys started putting bills in the slot and she stripped slowly, did some more stuff with the pole, and finally lowered herself into a Lucite tub. She soaped up, got out, and writhed around for a few minutes. Then she rinsed off and dried herself for what seemed like a year and got dressed again. The poor woman has to do that over and over every day for hours." It was clear from Illuminada's tone that she would not have found such repetitive work gratifying.

"Maybe it's not your thing, girlfriend, but she looked really into it," said Betty. "She seemed to be enjoying every minute of her routine. I wonder if she was faking that." Betty poured the last of her shake from the metal container into her glass.

"Did she use real weights, do you think?" Vic asked. "If she did, she must be one strong stripper, from all those reps."

Ignoring Vic's comment, I said, "You know, the club's website is out of date. The room listed as Big Apple Academy isn't there. I bet that's where Eunice performed. I bet she entertained men who fantasized about getting it on with their profs."

"Oh, you mean like my good buddies Sol and Raoul?" said Vic. "You wouldn't believe the stuff they tell me . . ."

"Must be a lot like what we hear from our good friend Betty, who's had this kinky thing about undertakers for years . . ." said Illuminada, too tired to resist this old line that we had been enjoying ever since Betty and Vic got together.

"Well, you can sit here all night comparing fantasies. I'm going home. I've got a nine o'clock class to teach tomorrow."

"So *chiquita,* I guess that means you didn't

see anything or anybody besides those two refugees from RECC that might lead to Eunice's killer?" Illuminada reminded me of the question she had posed earlier.

"Not that I know of. But I'm going back to that place. And I'm going alone." I stood as Betty signaled for the check. Before any of them could protest, I continued. "I'm going to contact the manager and see if he'll connect me with a woman in the chorus there who is about Eunice's size. I'm going to give her Eunice's costumes and see what I can learn from her."

"How are you going to contact the manager, *chiquita?* Do you even know who the manager is? The website didn't mention one by name," said Illuminada. She sounded peeved.

"Yes. I looked in Exotic Dancers Directory." I was proud of this triumph of research. "Not for nothing did I earn a Ph.D. I really do know how to find things out. His name is Michael Ackerley and he owns the club."

CHAPTER 16

To: Bbarrett@circle.com
From: Anncalicon@earthlink.net
Re: Kitchen makeover
Date: 10/31/01 11:24:18

Dear Down and Dirty in Hoboken,

I know where you're coming from on the kitchen renovation, believe me. I'm still in recovery from ours. Drew and I moved into our handyman's special in the early 70s. Our olive green appliances (remember that color? It was like something the cat would cough up after eating the spider plants) were already vintage. The oven was two steps removed from a campfire, and the sink, but don't get me started on the sink. Let's just say it made the village well seem high tech.

Drew was not into replacing these dinosaurs. He always said our appliances were made back when appliances were intended to last, not to be jettisoned for shoddier new models with trendy bells and whistles. I used to pray that our fridge would give out, but we only had that one problem with it on our daughter's wedding day. Thank God the caterer was able to replace the spoiled canapés during the ceremony. We didn't get a dishwasher until my parents died and left us theirs because Drew insisted dishwashers wasted water.

So how did I convince Drew to renovate our kitchen? I didn't. It was Nigella. You know, that sexy British babe who's always licking her fingers? The one on cable who in ten minutes whips up delicious goodies that would take you or me a year? Anyway once Drew started actually using the kitchen, well you don't have to be a rocket scientist to know that he wasn't going to put up with an oven that had three temperatures, burn, char, and disintegrate. And the fridge? All of a sudden he wanted a freezer bigger than a lunch box, one with a real crisper instead of a drawer full of water. Our sink was no longer adequate either. He really needed a double sink. And better storage space. Suddenly we had to have new cherry cabinets and marble countertops. And a dishwasher.

You get the idea. The old stuff was good enough for me to make three meals a day for him and three kids for nearly three decades, but not good enough for him. The renovation lasted two noisy, dirty, kitchenless years and cost upward of

$80,000 not counting the cost of take-out and marriage counseling, Now that I don't cook anymore, I have my dream kitchen.

Sour grapes in Sonoma

She wasn't the only sour grape in the jelly jar. I was feeling pretty rancid myself, especially after Ed showed up the morning after my visit to the Big Apple Peel. He had arrived flushed and fuming. "I hate to tell you, Professor. Our windows didn't get here yet, and when I called the manufacturer, he told me they might be held up as much as a week." Ed's use of the first person plural possessive indicated the extent to which he identified with his clients. He clearly felt our pain. He glanced at my face to see how I was taking news of yet another delay. What he saw did not reassure him. "Don't worry, Professor. I got plenty to do until they come. I got a lotta work yet on these cabinets." Ed gestured in the direction of his sawhorse and the assorted crude wooden constructs scattered around it. "I just figured you oughta know. And Sol too. He up yet?"

"Morning, Ed." Sol's appearance precluded my attempt to thank Ed for keeping me updated on the latest roadblock holding up our renovation. After a hug from Sol, I left the two of them standing there, debating whether or not it would do any good for Sol to call the window company himself and complain. "I mean if they say one week's delay, maybe they really mean three or four," said Sol, reciting one of the realities of home improvement we had discovered long ago.

"You can call if it'll make you feel better. But it won't do no good. If they're backed up, they're backed up is what I think." Ed's reasonable but frustrating pronouncement echoed in my ears as I left home in search of a chocolate croissant and the relative peace and order of my classroom.

In a startling feat of compartmentalization I managed to banish all thoughts of my disemboweled kitchen and focus instead on preparing for the Faculty Development Seminar, which was meeting that afternoon. I prepared a minilecture on effective conferencing, Xeroxed a relevant article, and planned how I would structure the seminar itself. This was to be the first time the group would meet without Eunice. Sadly, I remembered Nelson's request to eulogize her. I still hadn't gotten back to him. Annoyed with myself for not responding to a student's e-mail, I decided to let Nelson deliver the eulogy he had prepared. Maybe something in his demeanor would shed light on his relationship with Eunice. And after his reading, we could have a moment of silence dedicated to Eunice's memory.

Before the afternoon seminar met, I taught

169

two back-to-back speech classes and ate most of a container of yogurt on my way to class. I ferreted through my purse until my fingers made contact with the bulge of a bag of M & Ms. This might just be an M & Ms afternoon, one when I popped those little chocolate suckers into my mouth by the handful in order to stay alert. I figured there would be few trick-or-treaters this year, so it didn't matter if I dipped into the Halloween candy before it became officially left over, a new low even for me.

Nelson was waiting for me outside the classroom where the seminar met. He looked appropriately grave in a jacket, a tie, and dark pants instead of the Soprano Safaris T-shirt and chinos he usually wore to work. I was touched. I guess he had assumed he had my permission to address the group. Before he greeted me, I said, "Nelson, forgive me for not getting back to you. I hope you're still willing to read your eulogy. It will help all of us come to terms with our loss." He nodded solemnly.

Later, when most of our colleagues had arrived, I said, "As you know, we have lost a member of our group, Eunice Goodson. She was assaulted and killed on her way home from work last weekend." When I made this dramatic pronouncement, Barbara raised her head and Dinesh lowered his. Their expressions were solemn. But nobody registered the slightest surprise, which confirmed my sense that Eunice's murder was by now common knowledge at RECC. "Eunice and Nelson were writing partners, and he has written a eulogy for her. Let's give Nelson our attention, and when he finishes, I'd like us to share a moment of silence in Eunice's memory. Then if anyone else cares to speak, she or he may do so."

Nelson stood and made his way to the front of the room, where he paused for a moment to unfold the paper on which he had written his talk. Then in a voice that was slightly too loud for eulogizing Eunice to our small group but probably just right for explicating Soprano country to a busload of tourists, Nelson read what he had written. "Eunice Goodson has been taken from us. Now she is in a better place. As you remember, she was my writing partner." Here Nelson paused and raised his eyes from the paper he held in front of him so he could make fleeting eye contact with several of us before he continued. "So I had the privilege of reading her introductory essay. And I learned some things about Eunice that gave meaning to her short life and underscore the tragedy of her death." Nelson paused again and looked at us over the edge of his paper. So far, except for the decibel level, he was doing well. As he continued, I found it almost impossible to imagine that he might have stabbed Eunice to death. "Eunice left her family when they didn't support her desire for education and her driving ambition to become an anatomy teacher. She worked hard at a demanding and demeaning job to put herself through undergraduate and graduate school so she could gain the knowledge she would need."

I hoped he wasn't going to trash Eunice's club work anymore. That would detract from the point he was making about her dedication and determination. I needn't have worried. When he continued, Nelson said, "And here at RECC, she was trying to be the best teacher she could even though, as a part-timer, she didn't earn much money. Her students and colleagues will miss her. Let us all take comfort in the knowledge that Eunice has found peace in a place where someday she will be reunited with her family and where she can teach as she always dreamed she would, secure in the knowledge that God has forgiven her all her earthly sins."

When Nelson had described the vision of Eunice finding forgiveness in heaven, which ended his tribute, he lowered his head, our signal to sit in silence for a moment. My inner speech teacher checked in unbidden, but irrepressible, to evaluate the content and delivery of Nelson's talk. *Kind of a holier-than-thou ending*, I thought, *and loud enough to wake the poor dead woman herself, but not bad on the whole.* Before I could mentally assign him a grade, Nelson took his seat, and I stood and asked for additional comments.

No one came forward. I thanked Nelson and began handing out the article on faculty-student conferencing that I'd Xeroxed. I delivered my lecture and then divided the group into pairs to role-play conferences. One member of each pair was to assume the role of a student doing poorly at midsemester, The other was to act as the faculty member attempting to help the failing student define and work on whatever was impeding his or her progress.

As I made my way from pair to pair, I overheard Barbara saying, "I don't think there's anything demeaning about stripping. My college roommate was a club dancer for years. That's how she put herself through law school."

Good for Barbara, I thought. I wondered why she hadn't spoken out earlier. I'd found Nelson's eulogy a little sanctimonious myself. But he was the only one who had taken the time to prepare anything and probably the only one of the group who had known Eunice well enough to miss her. Pulling a chair over to where the two sat, I said, "You two can finish this interesting debate over coffee later on. For now, I'd like you to work on the task I assigned. Who wants to play the student first? Nelson?"

173

By the time I moved on, they were involved in a simulated conference, and Barbara was inquiring, "But, Nelson do you see any connection between your six absences and your poor grade on the exam?" I congratulated myself on having role-modeled a gentle but effective professorial intervention.

CHAPTER 17

To: Bbarrett@circle.com
From: Tjenkins@juno.com
Re: Eunice's costumes
Date: 11/01/01 06:32:24

Dear Ms. Barrett:

I work at the Big Apple Peel and Michael Ackerley suggested I contact you about Eunice Goodson's costumes. I wear the same dress, bra, and pants size Eunice did, and I'd sure appreciate having her outfits. I don't have the same shoe size, but there's a dancer here, Melanie Melnick, who thinks she does and who'd like to try on Eunice's shoes and boots. Mel and I would be happy to come to Hoboken to pick up these items, but Michael says you prefer to deliver them to us personally at the club. Next week I'll be getting off work at 6 and could meet you there at that time. Melanie gets through at 7 this week and next. What would be a good night for you to come? Once we've made a date, I'll give you directions and alert Daphne our hostess so she can bring you backstage.

Thanks very much for deciding to give Eunice's stuff to a club dancer. That's a nice thing to do and most people wouldn't think of it. I didn't know Eunice too well, but I think she'd have liked that.

Sincerely,
Tiffany Jenkins, R.N.

Thanks to my Exotic Dancers Directory I hadn't had any trouble contacting Michael Ackerley, owner and manager of the Big Apple Peel. In fact, when I called, he picked up the phone himself. "Mr. Ackerley, I'm a friend of Eunice Goodson's." I paused a moment, curious to see how he would respond when I mentioned Eunice.

Just as I was wondering if her murder had even made the New York papers, he said, "Yeah. Terrible what happened to her. Terrible. I'm sorry. The cops were here, or I wouldn'a known what happened to her. Nice kid, she was. I'm sorry," he repeated.

"Thanks," I said. "Well, I'm disposing of her property and it occurred to me that rather than give her costumes to Goodwill, I might give them to another dancer, someone her size who could use them. Is there a dancer at your club about Eunice's size?"

"Sizes are a little outta my league," he said. "But just hold on a minute, will ya?" I heard him call out, "Daphne, come here. Is Tiffany the same size as Eunice, would you say? Or does Natasha come closer?" There was a pause. "Some friend of Eunice is on the phone. She wants to give Eunice's costumes to one of the dancers."

Daphne must have cast her vote with Tiffany, but I didn't learn that until later. When Michael Ackerley spoke to me again, he said, "Yeah. I got a girl here who could wear Eunice's stuff. And she'd be glad ta have it too. Thing is though, I don't give out my girls' names. And especially not now. Not after what happened. But if ya give me your phone number or even your e-mail address if ya got one, I'll have her contact ya."

I complied with his request. "Thanks. After she gets in touch with me, I'll bring in the clothes and give them to her personally," I said.

"Whatever." Michael Ackerley was clearly not too interested in the details of this transaction. "And like I said, I'm sorry about what happened ta Eunice. I gotta say this for her. She never pulled a no-show, never came late. She could hustle more drinks in half an hour than five other girls workin' overtime. And she brung in repeaters. We called 'em teachers' pets." He paused before uttering his final tribute to Eunice. "That girl was a real pro." His words left me with a sour taste in my mouth. Nelson had viewed Eunice as a sinner, and Michael Ackerley saw her as a moneymaking machine. Somehow neither of these men's words evoked the Eunice Goodson I had known, and that saddened me.

Sol didn't want to meet me in New York after I dropped off the costumes, even when I suggested that we might feast on mussels and frites washed down with dark Belgian beer at one of his favorite eateries in the West Village. "Sol, we should eat in the city, spend a little money there. The restaurants are really hurting, especially the ones downtown."

"Not tonight, Bel. I just feel like Chinese take-out. I'll save you some," he said. Now there's nothing wrong with Chinese take-out, but we'd eaten a lot of it since Ed had transformed our kitchen into a demolition site. What Sol really meant was "I'm afraid to go to Café Bruxelles because a terrorist might blow it up while I'm indulging my passion for mussels with good beer and those incredible frites with vinegar . . ." I tried to stifle the recurring thought that my beloved might never recover from his PTS, that he would live a life limited and defined by fear. This specter both enraged and alarmed me. Forcing this particular scenario into a compartment all its own in the furthest recesses of my mind, I shrugged my shoulders and set out alone.

Felice had folded the costumes in tissue paper and packed them carefully in two enormous Wedding Central shopping bags. I'd e-mailed Tiffany that her friend Melanie would have to wait for the shoes until I made another trip. I walked the few blocks from the subway briskly. Visiting the Big Apple Peel as myself felt more comfortable than visiting in the guise of a horny Russian musician. Being slightly familiar with the place helped too. This time, when confronted by the greeter, whom I now knew to be named Daphne, I said, "Hi, Daphne. I'm Bel Barrett. I have an appointment with Tiffany Jenkins at seven. She said you'd take me to her."

The exaggerated smile I recognized from the other night disappeared from Daphne's face as her features reassembled themselves into a frown and then a very slight and crooked grin. "You're Eunice's friend," she said, in a voice that was surprisingly soft, its girlishness at odds with her truly remarkable cleavage and layered makeup. She reached out and tapped my arm lightly with her squared mauve fingernails. "OhmiGod, you've brought her costumes," she added, taking the bags from me and peering into one of them. "Come on in, Tiffany's expecting you." Daphne led me through the club's main room past the bar and dancers and through an unmarked door I'd not noticed on my earlier visit. The deafening music prohibited conversation, but once the door shut behind us, Daphne turned to me and said, "Now that she's got Eunice's costumes, maybe Tiff'll take over the Professor's solo gig." I quickly concluded that the Professor was Eunice's stage name. This mental leap was validated when Daphne added, "Eunice worked a room here called the Big Apple Academy. Thanks to her it was one of our most popular tourist destinations."

Daphne had not cracked a smile when she uttered that last line, so I stifled mine. Then in the hope of getting her to talk more about life at the Big Apple Peel, I said, "I never saw her dance. What was Eunice's routine like?" Daphne's response was disappointing. "Ask Tiff, why don't you? She's over there changing, the one with the scarves on her head. I've got to go back and mind the store." And with another pat on my arm, Daphne was gone, leaving me to approach a woman dressed as Vermeer's famous portrait, perhaps the same woman I had seen dance on my last visit. Several other dancers were changing into and out of costumes as I walked through the dressing room.

Tiffany was removing her identifying headdress. "Tiffany? I'm Bel Barrett, Eunice's friend." She smiled, draped her scarves over a convenient chair, and extended a hand. She motioned me to sit down on a stool in front of a counter cluttered with makeup, hair spray, deodorant, breath mist, and glitter.

"You know, seeing all this, I realize I didn't bring the things in Eunice's drawers or her makeup. I just brought what was in her closet. If you like, I'll get all that stuff together and bring it when I deliver the shoes," I said, looking at Tiffany.

"Damn straight, I'd like it. I've got student loans to pay back, so the less I have to spend right now, the better," Tiffany said. She was a chesty sandy-haired woman in her twenties. Like Eunice, she was solidly built and attractive without being drop-dead gorgeous. "You've no idea how costly all this can be." Tiffany gestured around the room at the brightly colored gowns folded over chairs and the ubiquitous vials, sponges, and tubes. "These duds may look as if we raided Woolworth's for them, but they cost, believe me."

"I believe you," I answered.

Just as I was straining to think of a subtle way to get her to talk about Eunice's life at the Big Apple Peel, a bevy of dancers trouped in followed by a turbanned dark-skinned woman in her forties wearing jeans and a black sweater. She appeared to be chastising the dancer just in front of her. Her crisp British accent contrasted with her casual attire and added credence to her rebuke. "I told you what happened to your check for last week, duck. You missed two shifts. You don't get paid if you don't dance. If you got a problem with it, have a chat with Mike.

181

He'll tell you the same thing. But you might listen to him."

"That's her ladyship, Amanda. She's our house mom, but we call her Queenie because of her accent and because she really gets off on bossing us around," said Tiffany, a good-natured smile brightening her face. Although I nodded, I must have looked bewildered at this explanation, because Tiffany continued talking as she pulled on a pair of gray cords. "Queenie schedules our shifts, keeps track of no-shows, and makes sure we have the cosmetics and other stuff we need. Her bark's a lot worse than her bite, so some girls try to get over on her, but she's pretty sharp. She and Eunice used to go at it something fierce," Tiffany said, buttoning the work shirt she had just put on and beginning to throw things into a large bag she had taken out of a locker behind her.

"I'd like to hear more about that," I said. "Can I buy you a cup of coffee or a beer?" I barely heard Tiffany's response because Queenie had stopped to chat with a girl who had just arrived, stripped out of her street clothes, and begun to pour red glitter into a cup to which she was also adding a liquid. Into this concoction she squirted something from a bottle clearly recognizable as Elmer's Glue. While I gaped, she stirred the mixture with a Q-tip and then swabbed it all over first one nipple and then the other. Voilà!

Noticing my slack-jawed stare, Tiffany smiled and said, "That's a trade secret. Ever want to gild your lilies, so to speak, just mix liquid latex, glitter, and glue. See? Now she's going to let it dry for five minutes, and then she's ready to join the others in the line. They do a number featuring red and blue nipples with white G-strings. It's patriotic, you know." She shrugged.

"I ought to spring for the tea just to thank you for bringing me these costumes. How about that? My treat, okay?" I nodded. Suddenly I was relieved that Sol wasn't waiting for me at Café Bruxelles. It might take a while to get Tiffany to tell me what I wanted to know. I followed her through a door at the side of the dressing room and onto the street.

"So why were Eunice and Queenie at odds?" I asked. "Mike said Eunice was a model employee."

"She was and she wasn't. Eunice wanted us to organize like in that documentary a dancer in San Francisco made." I favored Tiffany with another blank look. I was beginning to be embarrassed by how much I didn't know about this business. But Tiffany was very tolerant. *"Live Nude Girls Unite!"* she said. "Great film. You might like it. It's about how the dancers at a club in Frisco unionized."

"Oh, I can see how Mike might find that

disturbing. He's the owner and manager, right?" I asked. Tiffany nodded and turned to lead me into a deli. I noted the standard display, platters of glutinous-looking take-out food representative of at least six different cuisines, and a wall fridge holding canned and bottled beverages. Tiffany helped herself to a plastic container of California rolls and an iced tea. I opted for an iced tea.

"Doesn't what happened to Eunice make you anxious about your own safety?" I asked.

"It was kinda creepy," said Tiffany, managing to articulate clearly around a mouthful of seaweed, rice, and fake crab legs. "But it happened so far from here, in New Jersey, for God's sake, that we figure it was somebody from there or maybe somebody on the same train, a nut case or a junkie, you know." Like many New Yorkers, Tiffany uttered the name of my native state as if it were located on a distant galaxy rather than a fifteen-minute subway or bus ride away. "Maybe it was even somebody from her day job," said Tiffany. "I mean one of her students could have had a grudge, you know?"

"Gee, I was thinking the opposite," I said. I was amazed at how easy it had been to lead Tiffany into this conversation. Tiffany's eyebrows arched above the California roll suspended between her chopsticks. "I figured there might have been some patron of the club, some weirdo who liked her and followed her home or maybe somebody who hated her, another dancer or even her boss."

Tiffany grinned. "Eunice had the most regulars of all of us, you know, guys who came to see her a lot. We called them teacher's pets because they just paid their money, bought a drink, and went right into the Academy to check out the Professor. They were good tippers too." *Had Nelson Vandergast been one of Eunice's teacher's pets? Had he intruded on Eunice at her day job? Or had he been a welcome member of her coterie, a big tipper perhaps?* Although these questions were racing around in my head while Tiffany was talking, I decided not to pose them to her just yet. I had homework to do first. "Apparently a lot of guys really get off on the idea of a naked prof, especially one who raps their knuckles," she said, still smiling.

"Tell me about Eunice's dance routine," I said, my hand moving instinctively to the neckline of my shirt as if to button the top button.

"Oh she'd come in wearing her cap and gown and her glasses and carrying books and a ruler. Then she'd stand at a dais in front of a blackboard, take off her cap, and shake out her hair. Gradually she'd dance out of her gown, and she'd just be wearing a sexy slip and bra and panties underneath. Then she'd dance out of those. She used a lot of different songs too, including that kids' song

"No More Pencils, No More Books," but once she got down to her G-string, she'd dance to "Teach Me Tonight" and pretend to rap the knuckles of the guys sitting at the desks in the front. Did I mention that the guys sat at desks in the Academy?" I shook my head, trying to imagine the proper and rather serious Eunice Goodson I remembered cavorting around practically naked playing school.

"It's hard to imagine Eunice doing that," I said. "She was usually pretty serious."

"We're all pretty serious," said Tiffany. I thought she sounded angry, as if she were tired of explaining herself and her work to people. "In my day job I'm a visiting nurse. I dance to pay back my loans before I need home care myself and because it's fun."

"It seems like pretty hard work to me," I said. "Do you really enjoy it?"

Tiffany continued, "Well, think about it. In our day jobs most of us do what we're told, stress out a lot, and don't make much money. We can't control the outcome of what we do. Lots of my patients suffer and die." I nodded. Tiffany was probably relieved that finally I seemed to understand what she was saying, so she took my nod as an invitation to continue. "And we have family problems. We feel powerless. Let's face it, we are pretty powerless in this world we live in. And the terrorist attack didn't help." She jerked her head in the direction of the river and the wound in the city where the Towers had stood.

I nodded again. "Amen," I said.

"But dancing has a lot going for it. First of all, the pay isn't bad. Second, it's great exercise. And third, like I said, it's fun. When I see these guys gaping at me, I feel powerful, in control. It's really an awesome feeling. When I've had a bad day at work I like to come here and dress up and pretend I'm somebody else, somebody who can make people do what I want," she said, carefully placing some pickled ginger on her last California roll. "And you know what else? I've been dancing for a couple of years now, and I've made some really good friends. I was a bridesmaid in Melanie's wedding last year. We're totally close."

"Somehow I never thought of it the way you describe it. I guess I'm still hung up on the old feminist argument that stripping objectifies women and makes it easier for men to abuse them," I said. "Eunice and I used to argue about that." Mentioning our dead friend jolted me back to the reason Tiffany and I were having this tête-á-tête. If I wasn't careful, I'd get on my soapbox and never get anything else out of Tiffany that might help me to find Eunice's killer.

CHAPTER 18

Dear Prof B and Sol,

The good news is the windows are coming tommorow. Late in the day. The guy called me today and left word. The bad news is I got jury duty coming up day after tommorrow. I forgot all about it. I'll try to get done as much as I can before I go and maybe they won't pick me. I'll tell them I'm a teacher (ha ha). Ed

"Jury duty!" I exclaimed when I got home and Sol handed me Ed's note. I surveyed the kitchen and adjacent living-dining room. The whole place looked the way it had for several months, like a makeshift squatter's hovel *after* the wreckers broke it up. I began to entertain thoughts of moving to a hotel for the duration of this interminable and ill-advised project. "Oh God, Sol, I know it's petty of me to complain about this mess only a month or so after thousands of innocent people were killed and with poor Eunice dead, but I honestly don't know if I can survive in this chaos another day, let alone for weeks and weeks more. What if Ed's picked to serve on the jury for some case that drags on for months?" It was then, just as I articulated that entirely feasible possibility, that what Rebecca and Mark would call my "meltdown" occurred. I cradled my head in my arms, leaned on the filthy banister, and began to weep.

"You didn't eat yet, did you?" Sol asked, standing next to me at the foot of the stairs and patting my heaving shoulders. "I saved you some chicken with eggplant and brown rice. There may even be a shrimp dumpling or two with your name on it. Come on, Bel," he said, taking my hand and hauling me to my feet. "I'll nuke it and bring it upstairs. Just call me room service. After you eat, you can tell me all about your latest visit to that club."

Even in my teary state, I was reassured to see that Sol's PTS had not totally diminished his ability to relate to me. He remembered that without regular feeding, I am ill equipped to cope with life's challenges, and that I am not averse to occasional pampering. He also knew that if there was anything that could distract me from the prospect of an indefinite stay in that house of horrors we called home, it was the chance to rehash my latest sleuthing experience in front of a willing audience.

"So you didn't get to ask her specifically about that adjunct? What'shisname?" Sol asked as I finished recounting my conversation with Tiffany.

"Nelson Vandergast. No, but as I told you, I'm planning to go back with Eunice's cosmetics and her shoes, and then I'll bring a photo of him. I'm going to arrange a group photo of the Faculty Development Seminar or something so I can get the dancers and Daphne to see if they recognize him. Maybe he was a regular. Maybe he fell for Eunice and blamed her for having led him into a life of sin." I carefully lowered to the floor the tray holding the now empty take-out cartons.

"Yeah, he wouldn't be the first guy who abandoned his principles when enticed by a really attractive woman," Sol said. "I know something about that," he added with a wink.

"Right," I said, rolling my eyes at Sol's effort at gallantry. I was glad to see a vestige of his roguish humor, however hokey. He looked relieved to see that I was no longer in tears. "Seriously, I suppose it is possible that Nelson got it on with Eunice and then felt guilty for having been intimate with a woman whom he perceived as so degraded. Of course he'd blame her for his fall from grace and then have to kill her," I said, thinking out loud. "But good grief, Sol, the man leads a tour of Soprano sites," I mused. "Can he really be such a saint?"

"Who knows? You read about these guys who kill hookers all the time. Same kinda

190

thing," Sol said. "You were foresighted to set up a return visit to the club, and bringing the photo is a great idea too."

"I'm also going to try to learn more about that woman they call Queenie, and Mike Ackerley, the club owner. They both had bones to pick with Eunice," I added, feeling expansive after Sol's compliment.

He picked up the tray and set it atop one of the ubiquitous cartons that made our bedroom an exemplar of warehouse chic. "Want anything else?"

"No thanks, love," I answered. "And I'm sorry about that tantrum, but I really don't know how much more of this I can take."

"I know. It's not exactly my idea of home sweet home either," Sol said. "But maybe we'll sneak off to a B & B upstate this weekend. Should I go online and see what I can find?"

Even though I suspected that Sol was trying to lure me to the Hudson River Valley to look at real estate, I had to admit that his idea was appealing. "Can't hurt to look," I said, "but we can't really afford the freight right now, can we? Even so, it would be heavenly to be able to read student papers and prepare classes in a clean and orderly place." I fought and conquered the urge to kick the box nearest to me, the one on which the tray was balanced.

That night I dreamed of a jury of twelve

191

Ed lookalikes wearing carpenters' overalls sequestered in a B & B eating Chinese take-out by the carton.

Felice's breathless voice greeted me when I picked up the phone early the following morning. Her words tripped over one another. "Bel, I'm dropping Eunice's mail at your house on my way to work. I guess nobody told the post office she died, so the poor woman is still getting mail here. Gotta run now. Early fitting. Thank God people are getting married again." I picked up the manila envelope and threw it in my book bag as I left the house. It was probably all junk mail, but I'd go through it anyway and notify the post office that Eunice was dead.

All day at work and all weekend, I thought about Nelson Vandergast. I recalled the cold metal of the handcuff lying in Eunice's drawer. I thought some more about Nelson. His earnest manner and puritanical posturing could very well mask the twisted and repressed psyche of a killer, a killer who might enjoy handcuffing a woman to a bedpost or, for all I knew of such things, who might prefer to play the prisoner himself. The longer I thought about Nelson, the more plausible a suspect he seemed.

But I was determined to check out all our leads, so Monday when I got to my office, I called Illuminada. "Sorry to bother you with

192

this, but awhile back you said you were going to find out if the cops have followed up on Andrea Goodson, Eunice's sister, remember?"

"*Dios mío,* of course I remember. I just forgot to do it. So sorry. I keep trying to run a business here. Silly me. What can I be thinking? Let me get on it now, *chiquita.* It's just a phone call." And it must have been because in less than ten minutes Illuminada called back to say, "They can't even find Andrea Goodson, so they haven't questioned her. Do you want me to find her?" Illuminada took pride in her organization's ability to track down people. Her staff of investigators used state-of-the-art professional search software to good effect. She loved showing up the cops, who, with their outdated equipment and blundering bureaucratic moves, literally ate her dust.

"Sure. Go ahead," I said.

Illuminada got back to me in less than an hour. "The good news is Andrea Goodson's in rehab. The bad news is she's in a residential program for hard-core users where it's really tough to get access to her. They've got lots of rules about visitors and phone privileges and all that. You might have to become one of her long-lost relatives, *chiquita.* I think they do let family members in once in a while." The good news–bad news format of Illuminada's message had caused me to flash on Ed's similarly phrased missive and dis-

193

tracted me for a moment so that I almost missed the import of what my friend was saying.

"Hello. Bel, are you still there? Earth to Bel." I could tell from the pique in her voice that being ignored was not the response Illuminada had expected when she phoned me so quickly with this useful information.

"Yes, sorry. Thanks. That was really fast work. I didn't expect to hear from you for a few days at least," I said, trying to make up for my earlier rudeness. "I'll go talk to Andrea. Where is this place? In Manhattan?"

"Yes. She's in the Gotham Treatment Center, way over on East Tenth Street. Better call first to see who can get in to see her and when," said Illuminada. "I'm glad you're going to talk to her. Your Soprano tour guide may seem like the killer, but I bet on family every time. Besides, even if Andrea didn't kill her sister, she may have some idea who did. And if anyone can get it out of her, you can."

"Well, I'm going to try," I said, as always grateful when Illuminada validated my ability to get people to confide their secrets. "Who knows? Maybe there was a ghost in Eunice's past who came back to haunt her, and her kid sister knows who it is."

"Right, and you'll just go into Manhattan and ask her and she'll tell you and then you'll have him arrested. Case closed!" When we hung up, Illuminada and I were both chuckling at the improbability of the scenario she had laid out.

I was still smiling a minute later when the phone rang. "Sybil, since when don't you let me help you? It's okay for you and Sol to put me up for months and take care of me when I wasn't well after your dad died, but it's not okay for me to offer you a little hospitality. I guess I'm not a full citizen. Or maybe you think Sofia and I are too old to have guests? Well, we're not. Sofia and I want you and Sol to come here and stay for as long as you need to. You know we've got the grandkid room. I told you that when your renovation started, but you don't listen. It's not fancy, but it's clean and comfortable. And it's yours." My mother paused to take a deep breath.

I saw my opportunity to speak and seized it, knowing full well that another might not come along for a while. "Hi, Ma, let me get a word in here. I guess Sol told you about Ed getting called in for jury duty, right?" No slouch in the monologue department myself, I pressed on without waiting for her to reply. "Actually we're desperately hoping that he won't be picked, but if we could stay with you two for a few days, we'd really appreciate it." A visit with Ma and Sofia wasn't exactly a romantic getaway in a B & B with a river view, but it was free, and to refuse it now would provoke a volley of protests and accusations I wasn't up to rebutting. Besides, Sofia and Ma's place boasted genuine period décor, including a scarcely used parlor evocative of the formal fifties, a kitchen in which June Cleaver might have been at home whipping up a meat loaf, and a den dominated by a vintage entertainment center housing a large-screen TV. There was even a theme room, at one time occupied by Sofia's visiting grandchildren, long since grown. The last time I looked, this accommodation was really a museum filled with artifacts crafted by Sofia's descendants, one of whom had harbored a fondness for sculpting dinosaurs well into late adolescence, as well as photos of the artists themselves at various periods in their lives.

When I put down the phone, I barely had time to gather my books and rush to class. It wasn't until much later in the day that I had a chance to open the envelope Felice had left containing Eunice's mail.

CHAPTER 19

Eunice, I'm sorry. I'm going into rehab next week. I have news from home. Can we meet over the weekend? I could come to the club Sat. nite. Andrea

This cryptic message scrawled on a postcard in a childish hand stood out among the solicitations from charities and her university's alumni association that made up Eunice's mail. All of it, I noted, had been forwarded from a Manhattan address where, presumably, she had lived before relocating to Hoboken. On the front of the vintage card postmarked 09-15-01 was a photo of a few cows in a field beside a barn. Perhaps because it was rendered in black and white, this scene evoked the bleak, rather than the bucolic, aspects of rural life. After digesting the card's implications, I put it back in the manila envelope and reached for the phone.

"Gotham Center. How may I direct your call?" The female voice was mechanical, the off-putting drone of a gatekeeper.

"I'd like to speak to the social worker or therapist working with Andrea Goodson, please," I said in that tone of voice I reserved for telling students to revise a paper if they expected a grade on it. It was a voice that got results.

"And who may I say is calling?" the gatekeeper asked, apparently unimpressed.

"Bel Barrett," I replied, knowing that she would require more specific information.

"Are you a relative, Ms. Barrett?" Predictably, the gatekeeper, exuding false patience, pressed me.

"I'm a friend of the family," I replied, growing weary of this dueling dialogue. "I'll elaborate on my relationship to the Goodsons to Ms. Goodson's caseworker or therapist."

"That'll be Ms. Markey," the voice said, sighing audibly. Clearly I had exhausted even her false patience. Having failed to discourage me, she was eager now to be rid of me. "Please hold while I transfer you to Ms. Markey's voice mail."

Mentally composing an appropriate message to leave in the limbo of voice mail, I was surprised to hear a human on the other end of the phone.

"Linda Markey here. How may I help you?" This woman sounded genuinely curious. Clearly hers was not the voice of a gatekeeper but rather of someone both educated and inclined to be helpful.

"Ms. Markey, I'd like to visit with Andrea Goodson. I was a close friend of her sister, and I have some disturbing news that I'd like

198

to deliver to her personally," I said. Even though Illuminada had encouraged me to masquerade as a relative in order to gain access to the fortress that was the Gotham Treatment Center, I'd decided to go with the truth, at least at first. My reasoning was that, given the intergenerational hostility among the Goodsons, if Andrea heard that a relative was coming, she herself might refuse to see the visitor. Or, expecting a family member, she might reject me as a fake on sight and have me put out. I also had a feeling that unless Andrea had, in fact, lured her sister to a late-night meeting and stabbed her to death herself, she did not yet know of Eunice's murder. I wanted to tell Andrea of her sister's death myself and gauge her reaction.

"I see. You know we don't usually allow visitors during a resident's first week here, but Ms. Goodson has been with us at least that long, so there should be no problem in that regard. And we usually allow only relatives to visit first, but . . ." Here Ms. Markey hesitated ever so slightly, her commitment to confidentiality fleetingly at odds with her sympathy for Andrea who, I was sure, had had no concerned kin vying to visit. I could tell that Ms. Markey had decided that it could be good for Andrea to have a visitor. After all, she had endured the initial rigors of the Gotham program and was, presumably, drug free as a result. So it came as no surprise to me when Ms. Markey said, "Residents with privileges generally receive designated visitors between seven and nine p.m. Shall I leave a card with your name on it at the desk tomorrow? That would give Ms. Goodson a chance to process her anxiety about your visit in our group session tomorrow afternoon."

A visit to a possibly homicidal drug addict in a monastic treatment facility was not my idea of a fun-filled evening, but I wanted to see what I could glean from Andrea Goodson. "Yes. Tomorrow will be fine. Thank you for your cooperation."

After work the following afternoon I left a packed overnight bag and my book bag on the bed where Sol would find them and bring them with him to Ma and Sofia's later. I left food and water out for Virginia Woolf and taped a note for Ed on top of the huge stack of windows then occupying the spot where the sink-island of my dreams was supposed to go. As it turned out, he had been selected to serve on a jury hearing an accident case that, the judge estimated, would take no more than a week to try. Because he would be unavailable for at least five business days, Ed planned to work on our cabinets on Saturday. Thank goodness Ma and Sofia had offered us a weekend haven away from the din and dust of saw and sander.

Upon hearing that I was to be out for the

evening, Sol had invited Ma and Sofia to Tania's in downtown Jersey City for a Ukrainian feast. Never one to knowingly miss a meal, I'd decided to fortify myself on my way across Lower Manhattan with a bite to eat at the Second Avenue Deli. By the time I walked there from the PATH stop at Ninth Street and Sixth Avenue, I'd worked up an appetite and, more importantly, the justification for having a tongue sandwich with cole slaw on rye bread and, for dessert, some of the deli's incomparable chocolate babka. This is a bite to eat like a pizza is a canapé. But the Second Avenue Deli is one of the few places left, even in New York, where those of us who belong to the dwindling breed of tongue-sandwich aficionados can still get a really good one. And so I ate the whole thing. I didn't even toy with the notion of a doggie bag. Washing the babka down with a cup of tea, I was ready for my encounter with Andrea.

But I was too stuffed to walk the rest of the way across town and still arrive near seven o'clock. I hailed a cab easily on the nearly deserted street, and the driver whisked me through the eerily silent post–September 11 East Village to the door of the Gotham Treatment Center. This turned out to be an innocuous-looking three-story gray building, where a receptionist seated at a small table carefully monitored foot traffic. Ms. Markey had been as good as her word. An envelope containing a guest pass with my name and Andrea's on it was ready for me. I stuck the adhesive-backed pass onto my sweater, where it advertised to anyone who cared to look the fact that I was an approved visitor. "The residents receive guests in the all-purpose room, over there," the receptionist volunteered before I had a chance to ask. He pointed at a half-open door off the right-hand side of the lobby.

Although I'd spent a fair amount of time contemplating how I was going to handle my meeting with Andrea, I was not sure how I would recognize her. I hesitated at the door to the large room. Groups of mismatched chairs circling odd-sized side tables were scattered throughout, giving the place the shabby but not uncomfortable air of a flea market specializing in furniture. I stood in the doorway, eyeing the clusters of people and wondering if Andrea was among them waiting for me or if she herself had not yet arrived. I'd soon see. I stepped across the threshold and was nearly overcome by cigarette smoke. It seems that the Gotham Treatment Center was fortified against everything but tobacco, and almost everyone in the room was smoking furiously.

Reminding myself that tobacco is considered by some a lesser evil than other drugs, I strolled around the room, hoping Andrea would spot her name on my visitor's pass and claim me. But before that happened, I spotted her. With Eunice's square shoulders and chin and Eunice's dark eyes and hair, she looked like a much slighter and decidedly less busty version of her sister. Like Eunice, Andrea wore glasses. But where Eunice had dressed in simple clothes in dark and neutral shades, Andrea wore an orange corduroy cowboy shirt with silver buttons over rust-colored pedal pushers and bright green rubber clogs. Eunice had always seemed composed, but as I approached Andrea, I could feel the nervous energy that animated her face and eyes. At irregular intervals her features seemed to shift like the shards of glass in a kaleidoscope.

She stood with several other people who, I assumed, were also residents expecting visitors. They huddled next to a paper-covered table laid with cookies, cider, popcorn, apples, and an urn of coffee and beneath a poster listing the twelve steps to a drug-free life. Like wallflowers at a mixer, they cast nervous glances at the door as they chatted. I walked over to Andrea, my hand extended. "Andrea Goodson? I'm Bel Barrett." Reflexively she extended her own hand, a collection of small cold bones at the end of a thin arm. A sliver of white gauze bandage was bright against the cuff of her orange sleeve. She nodded and withdrew abruptly from the triad of other residents. "Can we take those seats over there?" I pointed to a card table flanked by two chairs. Andrea nodded again. I was careful to appropriate the chair facing the center of the room, leaving her the one facing the wall where the light from the sconce illuminated her face.

"So, you're a friend of my sister's? She send you?" Andrea's voice was somewhere between a snarl and a growl. Her square chin jutted out as she spoke, turning her perfectly legitimate questions into challenges. Her hands clutched the arms of her chair so hard that her knuckles whitened. I waited a minute before I answered, noting again her spare and small-boned frame. Could this borderline anorexic have stabbed her much sturdier sister to death? Would drugs have given her added strength? Anger? The advantage of surprise? In the deepening silence, Andrea's left eye began to blink and then her right shoulder developed a decided twitch. Could this totally wired woman have been clever and focused enough to have devised a murder plot and carried it out?

"Andrea, your sister is dead." I studied her face, her hands. I listened.

"She is not," she said, in a tone somewhere between derision and denial. "She just moved to New Jersey a few months ago, that's all. She got pissed off at me for ripping her off, so she locked me out, packed up, and moved the first week in September. Leave it to my big sister to get out of Manhattan just before the shit hit the fan." Andrea shook her head in the time-honored manner of younger siblings continually confounded by the capability and prescience of their older brothers and sisters.

"Are you trying to find her?" she asked, suddenly helpful. "I've got her old address in Manhattan if you want it. They'll forward her mail for a year. What do you want Eunice for? Who are you anyway?" Without asking how I felt about it, Andrea eased a cigarette and a book of matches out of her shirt pocket and lit up in one practiced, effortless gesture. The familiar ritual seemed to steady her. The kinetic collage that was her face was momentarily at rest.

"Eunice Goodson really is dead, Andrea," I repeated. "Here, see for yourself." I pulled a copy of the article reporting Eunice's murder out of my purse and handed it to her. She took it and glanced at it. Then, drawn by the headline, she read it, oblivious of the ash forming on the end of her cigarette. I grabbed the ashtray on the table and stuck it under her little torch to catch the burning residue. Stubbing out the cigarette without lifting her eyes, Andrea reread the few columns of print. Handing it back to me, she took off her glasses and rubbed her eyes. I fought my inclination to hand her a Kleenex until I could see if she had actually teared up. She reached for another cigarette. This time she fumbled as she worked to extricate it. Unable to do so, she finally took the pack out of her shirt pocket, pried out a cigarette, and repocketed the pack. It took her two strikes to get the match lit, and then the tiny flame wavered in her trembling hand.

Not until she had inhaled deeply did Andrea look up. It was then, just before she exhaled a veil of smoke, that I saw the tears sliding silently down her cheeks. Her face was now as white as her knuckles had been earlier, and when she spoke, her voice was tight with the effort of suppressing sobs. I handed her a package of Kleenex and fought my own urge to put my arms around her. Trusting the cigarette to the ashtray temporarily, Andrea blew her nose, wiped her eyes, and reached for her glasses. Once she had them back on, she picked up her cigarette and took another deep drag. Then she said, "I'm sorry, but Eunie was my big sister, you know? She always tried to help me, even back home. She took plenty of beatings for me." Andrea's eyes filled anew, and she dabbed at them behind her glasses. "She gave me the money to get away from the farm, go to the university. But not me. I blew her off back then too. I took her money and came straight here." Andrea shook her head, now perhaps marveling that once she had wanted to come to New York.

"When Eunie finally graduated and came out here herself, she saw I had no steady job, just a little low-end temp work, you know? So she gave me a place to stay and tried to get me to go to school again. She sent for catalogs for me. She lent me money. She lectured me about my friends, about Enrique. She said he was a sadist." Andrea's voice was singsong as she listed Eunice's acts of sisterly devotion. "But I don't have to tell you. You were her friend. You know how she was." Andrea sighed and continued. "So anyway, when she saw I was doing drugs, she tried to get me to leave Enrique, go into rehab. She researched programs all over the city, you know. Back then I didn't want any part of that twelve-step shit." Andrea looked around and shrugged, as if acknowledging the irony of her present surroundings in view of her distaste for the rituals of rehab. "I repaid her for all this by ripping her off for money to get high." Again Andrea shrugged, but this time the gesture was self-deprecating. "And now it's my fault she's dead."

Following this last astounding statement, Andrea stubbed out her cigarette, crossed her forearms in front of her and grasped her elbows in her hands. Then she began to rock back and forth in her chair, tears oozing out from beneath her closed eyelids and coursing down her cheeks. She resembled every woman who had ever grieved, and before I could restrain it, my hand reached out to pat her clumsily on the shoulder. "I'm sorry, Andrea," I said.

After a few minutes had passed and she had swiped at her tears with a Kleenex I provided, I broke the silence. "Tell me, how do you figure it's your fault she's dead?" I used the gentle voice I saved for singing Abbie J to sleep.

Still rocking, Andrea began to talk through her tears. "After Eunie locked me out, I went to live with my boyfriend. Except Enrique wasn't really my boyfriend, he was my pimp, really, my supplier too, you know. And Eunie was right. He was a sadist. He used to tie me up . . ." My mind flashed on the handcuffs Felice and I had found in Eunice's drawer. In my feverish fantasy they had belonged to Nelson Vandergast, who had used them on Eunice, but maybe they were Andrea's, and her big sister had confiscated them in an effort to protect the younger woman from her brutal boyfriend.

Shaking her head as if to stave off a memory, Andrea continued. "Anyway, I'd turn tricks for money to get us both strung out. One night a trick I picked up at a bar turned out to be a dude from home, Eunie's old boyfriend, Will Carrington." Andrea stopped rocking, blinked her eyes open, and contracted her brow. "Would you believe? Out of all the thousands of Johns in Manhattan, I pick up my sister's old boyfriend?" To be sure that I got the point, she elaborated. "Will was playing hookey from some convention for lay ministers no less and hooked up with a hooker who turns out to be from his hometown. I mean how likely is that? I mean there have to be millions of pros in Manhattan, you know." She looked at me, expectantly, waiting for me to acknowledge the magnitude and absurdity of this coincidence. Aware that Andrea hadn't been in New York long enough to realize that at times, the big city is really just a small world, I nodded, as much to satisfy her as to ensure the uninterrupted flow of her narrative.

"Eunie would have just loved that," she mused. "Anyhow, I blew him off," she added quickly. "No way I was going to have sex with Will Carrington. Besides, he paid for my drinks and then some just for talking to him." Andrea shook her head as she recounted Will's odd behavior. "Wanted to know all about Eunie, what she was doing, where she worked, if she was still dancing, if she was married."

Andrea lit up another cigarette and inhaled. She seemed calmer. When she spoke next it was in a low voice from behind a cloud of smoke. "Right after that night Enrique, my boyfriend, beat me up real bad." Andrea put her hand to her face and caressed her jaw, as if recalling a blow. "That was when I sent

Eunie a card apologizing and asking her to meet me after work. I never heard back, but I went there anyway, to the club when I figured she'd be getting out. I hung around outside, but she didn't show. Maybe she left early to avoid me or . . . maybe she was already dead." Andrea began to rock again, silent now.

"I don't get it, Andrea. How does this make you responsible for Eunice's death?" In the hope of getting her to resume talking, I posed the question even though I suspected I knew the answer.

"Because I told that sick fuck Will Carrington the name of the club where Eunie worked. That's how."

CHAPTER 20

www.Sopranosafari.com
Can't get enough of Tony and Carmela and the gang on Sunday nights? Want to enrich your weekly viewing experience? Try a *Soprano Safari!* Kick back, relax, help yourself to a cannoli and a cappuccino or espresso, and enjoy a video-tour of Tony and Carmela Soprano's suburban New Jersey home while cruising down U.S. 1 & 9 on one of our plush air-conditioned buses. In Kearny you will check out the original inspirations for Big Pussy's Auto Body Shop and Satriale's Pork Store. After driving by a few favorite body drops in the Meadowlands, you'll disembark re-laxed and refreshed at Lodi's Satin Dolls, location for the Bada Bing (no photos al-lowed but T-shirts for sale) before heading for Elizabeth, N.J., and a visit to the social club rumored to be the model for Tony's. Later you will visit the waterfall in Paterson where a debtor of Tony's paid the ultimate interest on a loan. At each exciting au-thentic stop on this four-hour tour through Soprano country, your *Soprano Safari* guide will offer informative minilectures and an-

swer questions. Group rates and dinner tours available . . .

"Don't read the text! It's the head shot I want you to check out," said Betty, pointing to the smiling face of Nelson Vandergast. He stared at me from the printout that I had automatically begun to read. I passed it to Illuminada, who held it tightly against the breeze blowing in from the river. "I figured there'd be a website for his business, and if it featured a picture of this creep, you wouldn't have to bother staging a photo-op in your seminar. You can just flash this around at the Big Apple Peel and see if anybody there recognizes him as a regular of Eunice's." The self-satisfied expression Betty wore resembled that of my cat, Virginia Woolf, just after she deposited the mangled carcass of a fledgling robin at my feet one morning this past summer. I tried not to smile. It was obvious that giving me Nelson's photo clearly satisfied both Betty's need to be efficient and her equally compelling need to tell others what to do.

Even so, Betty had a right to be smug. I took her arm in mine for a moment as the three of us strode along the river walk in Hoboken. "Oh, thank goodness. It's a struggle to cover everything we need to in the seminar, so I'm delighted I don't have to make time to play photographer. But listen up! Maybe Nelson didn't kill Eunice. I visited Andrea Goodson the other night and she gave me a brand new lead to check out." Illuminada looked up from the printout.

"I bet she had to think fast to find someone to implicate so you wouldn't focus on her," said Illuminada. "No wonder she deflected your attention to another suspect."

"No. It's not like that. Andrea didn't stab her sister, but she feels responsible for Eunice's death nonetheless," I said.

"You lost me on that one, girlfriend," said Betty, pausing in front of the photo of a young man taped to the low wall to make a quick sign of the cross, something I'd never seen my devout Catholic friend do in public. She took my arm in hers again, and I squeezed it tight for a second as we resumed walking. I knew that dead young man's face had triggered her memory of those long hours when she had thought her own boy was dead.

Eager to distract her as well as to update her, I said, "Well, I went to the rehab center and chatted with Andrea for over an hour. She's a pitiful little thing, very anxious, and possibly suicidal," I said, remembering the flash of white bandage I'd spotted protruding from Andrea's sleeve. If Andrea hadn't slit her own wrists, she had an abusive boyfriend who probably would have ended her life before long.

"What did you expect, *chiquita?* Recovering addicts look either like waifs or whales," said Illuminada in her most judgmental tone. "And they're all nervous. After all, detox in a rehab center is not exactly a spa treatment." Illuminada had joined elbows with Betty, and, in spite of the difference in our heights, the three of us matched our strides. "Don't write her off as a suspect just because she's pathetic, Bel."

"I'm not." It irritated me when Illuminada, who prided herself on her objectivity, implied that I allowed my sympathy to influence my judgment, but I decided against making an issue of it. Instead I continued. "But listen, I really don't think Andrea even knew about Eunice's death. I had to show her the newspaper account of the murder to make her accept it, and then she wept real tears."

"What did she say about that postcard?" asked Betty. "Did she admit that she sent it?"

"Oh yes. She sure did, but that's not really the issue for her," I said. They both stopped walking and looked at me.

"Come on," I said, resuming our earlier pace. "I'll explain." We had reached the uptown Starbucks before I finished recapping my meeting with Andrea Goodson.

"Let me get this straight, girlfriend," said Betty, keeping her voice low so the other people in line wouldn't overhear. "Andrea

214

Goodson thinks Eunice's high school boy-friend, who is now a lay minister, went to the Big Apple Peel, waited for Eunice to come out, stabbed her to death, and then went back to his hotel, finished his conference, and returned to his upstate New York home?"

"You got it," I said, nodding. "The poor kid's all torn up about it. Thinks she should have realized that Carrington is a psychopath and that she never should have mentioned the name of the club." We placed our beverage orders and waited.

"*Dios mío, chiquita,* you are such a bleeding heart. You see a few tears and you totally lose perspective," said Illuminada, as we left the café, beverages in hand. This time it was a little harder to repress a defensive come-back, but once outside I managed it. The day was so unseasonably balmy that arguing seemed as great a travesty as remaining inside during lunch. After all, Illuminada was entitled to her opinion, and there were worse things to be accused of than being tender-hearted. We headed for the benches in a mini park between the newest high rise and the river.

"I think we have to check the guy out, but we also shouldn't forget that Andrea is still a suspect until she comes up with an alibi," said Illuminada.

"Don't forget, the tour guide is still plausible as a perp too," said Betty. "Bel, you

215

have to pass that photo around at the club."
It wasn't enough that one friend was accusing me of having a heart for brains, now
the other one was ordering me around. Betty
was born to command though, and one had
to get used to it or miss out on the many
other things she brought to her friendships.

"And, yes, *chiquita,* before you ask, I'll put
Will Carrington's name in my magic com-
puter and see what comes out," said
Illuminada.

"I'll go back and talk to Andrea again and
see if she has an alibi for the date Eunice
was killed as well as what date she actually
went to meet Eunice. Maybe she has an alibi,
and, better yet, maybe she saw somebody or
something. Who knows?" I said, sighing at
the thought of spending yet another evening
at the Gotham Treatment Center.

"Don't sound so martyred. This whole
thing was your idea, remember?" said Betty.
"And our tour guide is still plausible as a
perp too. You have to go back to talk to Tiffany and those others at the club and flash
this photo around. I wish I could help, but
you're the one who's established the contact.
You're the one they expect."

"I know, I know," I said. "Looking at the
bright side, frankly I'm glad of an excuse to
be away from home. Sol's still circling ads for
rural real estate and surfing the ads online
too. And it gets worse. Did I tell you Ed has

jury duty? He won't be able to work for at least a week."

"Oh no," Betty and Illuminada chorused.

"Yes. The whole house is a disgusting sty. We're staying with my mother and Sofia for a few days," I added.

"That's a good idea," said Betty. "Why don't you stay with them until the whole thing is over? I'm sure they love having you."

"Sol and I talked about it, but strange as it sounds, we'd rather go home for the week that Ed's not there. The house may be a mess, but at least we'll have some privacy. We don't get much of that when Ed's on the job or with Ma and Sofia fussing over us at their house."

"Why not stay with me and Vic?" Betty offered for at least the third time since our renovation had begun. "You'd have plenty of privacy, that's for sure. We're hardly ever home."

"You know you could stay with us," said Illuminada, not for the first time either. "But it wouldn't be too private. Not with Mamacita around." She grinned at the thought of her mother, who lived upstairs but whose powerful presence filled the house. "Raoul and I are still afraid to make a sound when we have sex. That woman can't hear anything when you sit across the table from her, but just try to keep something from her and . . . *caramba!* I swear, the walls at our house have ears."

"I know what you mean now," I said. "Sol and I can't even argue when Ed's there. Just when one of us is about to tell the other one off, the sander stops, and we have to pretend to be civil," I said. "And of course, we never argue in front of Ma and Sofia."

"Well, girlfriend, whenever you two lovebirds want to have a real knockdown dragout domestic dispute, just come right on over to our house," said Betty as the three of us tossed our cups into the trash can and linked arms to walk back to where Illuminada had left her car.

CHAPTER 21

To: Bbarrett@circle.com
From: Rbarrett@uwash.edu
Re: No way T-day in NY
Date: 11/07/01 09:08:02

Mom, don't get your undies in a wad, but there is no way in hell that Keith and I and Abbey J can get to upstate NY for Thanksgiving at Sol's daughter's house this year. Not to mention that we have planned for months that you guys were coming here, and we have invited eight (count 'em) holiday orphans who can't make it to where their families are. AND Mark and Aveda and Grandma Sadie are planning on coming. In fact, Aveda's blowing off her own family to come to our house to meet YOU. Grandma already bought their three tickets with some cash she won at roulette over the summer, remember? Oops! Silly me. I forgot you don't remember anything anymore. So when I got that e-mail from Sol inviting us to Alexis's for Thanksgiving, I felt really bad. Not for me or Keith because we can just chow down with the other orphans here, but your granddaughter, poor little Abbey J, has been making turkey place mats in her playgroup. The one she made especially for you has eyes made of M & Ms that she glued on herself. What's going on?

Love,
Rebecca

Rebecca's message greeted me when I got to my office at RECC on Monday morning. It was all I could do not to phone Sol, who was probably still at the table devouring a third helping of the French toast and maple syrup that Ma had painstakingly prepared for our breakfast. It's a good thing I restrained myself because at that moment I would have undoubtedly said something regrettable. Sol had known for months that we were going to Seattle for Thanksgiving that year. I recalled him saying that Alexis and Xhi had had plans to spend the day with his brothers and their wives in Rochester. In fact, just a few nights earlier I'd reminded Sol to go online to get our airline tickets. "Those tickets will be cheap now, I bet," was how I'd put it.

Sitting there sipping my tea and staring at Rebecca's e-mail message on the screen, I realized what lay behind Sol's attempt to relocate our Thanksgiving dinner to a venue three thousand miles east. A chill crept through my body until it reached my heart, freezing it. Sol, who used to think nothing of flying to Budapest for a breakfast meeting, no longer wanted to fly, was afraid to fly. Worse yet, he didn't want to tell me he was afraid, so he'd made this clumsy and transparent effort to avoid air travel by disrupting the holiday plans of several families. The poor guy. The poor airlines. Poor New York. Poor Washington. Poor America. Poor Afghanistan. Poor world. The weight of all this fear and suffering literally bowed my head, and that's why it was cradled in my arms on my desk when a rap sounded on my office door.

I sat up and opened the door. There stood Eduard Dupré, ready for his nine o'clock conference. My office hours had begun. There would be no time to consider the state of the world or the dubious progress of Sol's therapy until that evening after we had finished dinner with Ma and Sofia and returned home.

Conversation over dinner was not reassuring. "Sol says Alexis is making Thanksgiving this year and wants us all to go there instead of to Seattle," said Ma. There was nothing in her chatty tone to indicate that Sol's wish required a sudden change of carefully made plans. She wore her poker face too, the one she used to routinely take money from those foolish enough to call her bluff at the card table. As she spoke, Sol ran his fingers through his thinning hair, a gesture he made when under pressure.

"I heard. Rebecca e-mailed me about it this morning," I said quietly. Sol combed his hair with his fingers again, his eyes on my face.

"In all the confusion, I forgot to mention it to you. Isn't it a great idea?" Sol's usually deep voice sounded thin and reedy now.

"I guess we could use our plane tickets some other time," Ma said, passing the salad bowl to Sofia.

"We'll talk at home, Sol," I said, signaling Ma to drop the subject with a well-placed kick under the table. The kick was hard enough to get her attention, but not hard enough to damage her fragile shins. She glanced knowingly at me as she lowered a hefty portion of Sofia's manicotti onto my plate.

Sofia patted Sol's arm and said, "I know how you feel. I don't want to go to my son's house in Cleveland this year either. But I do want to go to the World Trade Center. You know, to see it for myself. To pay my respects. We both do. Maybe sometime you and Sol can drive us in . . ."

Sol, usually glad to chauffeur the Odd Couple wherever they wanted to go, didn't answer her except to say, "My compliments to the chef," and raise his glass of Chianti. "So how did your conferences and classes go, love?" he asked, changing the subject with what he knew was a question certain to elicit a lengthy response. Like most teachers, I found recounting in detail the challenges and rewards of my work-life a valuable, if somewhat longwinded, way of processing them. Ma and Sofia settled back in their chairs as I began with the story of Eduard Dupré and his emigration from Haiti after his parents' deaths. It was nearly nine when we said good night. Hugging Ma, I whispered directly into her hearing aid, "Don't change those tickets yet." She squeezed my arm, indicating that she had gotten my message.

"So Bel, I guess you're pretty pissed?" said Sol as we flipped on the light switch, illuminating the mess we called home.

"I was very angry until I realized that you're afraid of flying now," I said as gently as I could while skirting the stack of windows in the middle of the room. "I wish you'd told me about that too," I added. Sol pushed the fingers of both hands through his hair this time and said nothing. He looked beaten. "But I understand," I said. "That's why you're in therapy. I just hope you've discussed this with Dr. Sacks." One look at his guilt-stricken face and I knew that, for whatever reason, Sol had not chosen to share his fear of flying with his therapist either. "Cause you know, love, we might want to fly to Tahiti or someplace like that on our honeymoon," I said, leaning over the windows to plant a kiss on his neck. "Promise me you'll talk to her about it, okay?" He nodded. Later that evening I went online and made our flight reservations myself. My mother's daughter, I was taking a gamble. I was betting that Sol just couldn't stay this scared forever. Surely by Thanksgiving he'd be over the worst of his PTS.

It was with a sense of relief that I returned to Manhattan alone the next night carrying an oversized shopping bag of makeup and flamboyant underwear in one hand and a bag of equally glitzy footwear in the other. Even though I was no longer at all sure that Nelson Vandergast or any other regular of Eunice's had killed her, I found the prospect of a chat with Tiffany and her friend Melanie at the Big Apple Peel preferable to an evening at home. It was depressing to sit amid the piles of wood and windows watching the love of my life play FreeCell solitaire while tuned into the NPR news coverage that was the background sound of his new lifestyle. The hum of every low-flying Newark-bound plane caused him to twitch convulsively and turn up the volume on the radio.

"Let me help you," said a familiar voice close to my ear as I boarded the PATH train. The Good Samaritan turned out to be Marlene Proletariat, president of the Citizens' Committee to Preserve the Waterfront and an old friend of Sol's and mine. She and Sol had worked together on any number of campaigns to forestall greed-based overdevelopment of Hoboken's few swatches of riverside property. I handed her the lighter of my bags, and we claimed adjacent seats.

"Long time no see," said Marlene. "Haven't seen much of your sweetie either, come to think of it. In fact, I have to call him. He missed a meeting last week." I tried not to register either the surprise or dismay I felt at this news. Sol never missed CCPW meetings if he was in the country. Marlene chattered on, her dark curls bright against her red jacket. I'd almost forgotten how attractive she was. It seemed ages since that time when I had thought she and Sol had . . . but that was in another life. "We really need him to pitch CCPW to this new group in Hoboken." I widened my eyes, signaling my curiosity. "You know, it's funny. Hoboken's starting to draw retirees. They're buying condos and . . ."

Now I lowered my chin and furrowed my brow to indicate disbelief. In case Marlene couldn't read my expression, I said, "You've got to be kidding, Marlene. Why would grown-ups retire to this bedroom community for yuppies?"

"Think about it, Bel. You lived in the city until you had kids and then you exiled yourselves to the burbs while the little dears grew up. Now they have, and you've got an empty nest and a lot of time. You're not a golfer or a gardener. You sell the colonial house in Hackensack and move down here, where housing is still cheaper than across the river, but you can be in the city in ten minutes." I had to smile. To a born and raised Jerseyite, Manhattan would always be the city, no matter what. "Now you can take classes, go to galleries, shop, do the museums, the theaters, the concerts, the restaurants. Need I go on?" I shook my head. The jolt of the train stopping at Christopher Street threatened to topple the bag between my legs, so I clamped my knees together.

"What do you want Sol to pitch to them?" I asked.

"They've formed a small organization so they can get group rates for cultural events and have dinner together. Now they're looking for a local cause to support. They want to give back. Some of them have a little extra money. Some have connections at the state level. Most of them have time on their hands. The charter schools are hot for them, the hospital is courting them, the Arts Council has given them a private studio tour, and someone from the homeless shelter has met with them. But it would be really a coup if we could get them to make CCPW their pet project." Marlene's eyes glazed over for a moment as she contemplated what miracles could be wrought by converting this coven of geriatric culture vultures into champions of CCPW. "I've wangled an invitation for me and Sol to their next meeting, and I want to make sure he saves the date. Remember how he got that state grant for us? He can outpitch anybody including Fiona Farraday, that manipulating bitch from the Arts Council. He's got to go with me." Her voice was urgent. Marlene had no idea just how dysfunctional her prize spokesperson had become.

"I'm sure he will," I said, mentally crossing my fingers since I wasn't at all sure. But maybe Marlene could persuade him. I marveled, not for the first time, at her energy and commitment. I always felt exhausted after a conversation with her even though I seldom got to say much. As the train pulled into the Fourteenth Street station, I stood and Marlene handed me the bag that she had been holding on her lap. "Besides, it's a dinner meeting at a restaurant one of their kids cooks in. I forget the name of it. It's in the financial district. They're reopening, but they're really hurting, so the group's meeting there in a private room. It should be an interesting evening."

"Call him," I called over my shoulder as I elbowed my way out of the train and onto the platform. To myself I added, *Yes, Marlene. Call him, because if anything can get Sol going again, it's CCPW. He just might force himself to venture into the city if he thinks it will help CCPW. And once he can do that, he'll start to recover, I know it.* Tears had welled by the time I clambered up the stairs, and I had to put my burdens down for a moment to dab at my eyes with a Kleenex.

By the time I got to the Big Apple Peel, Tiffany was waiting at the door to the dressing room in her street clothes. She was chatting with a short, full-faced woman with the straight black hair of an Egyptian princess and the thin smile of an ice queen. I was only a minute or two late. "Hi, Bel. Here, let me take that," Tiffany said, relieving me of the two bags. "Bel, this is Melanie. Mel, Bel," she went on, giggling at the silly rhyme. Before Melanie and I could do more than shake hands, Tiffany said, "Bel, thanks for this stuff. Would you look at all this, Melanie? It's poor Eunice's whole works and her shoes." Melanie pulled her lime green wraparound chenille robe closed and approached the bag of shoes. "Come on. Leave those. You can try them on later. Get dressed. I told you, I made appointments for bikini waxes and we're going to be late," said Tiffany.

Disappointment dripping from each word, I said, "Oh no, I was hoping you'd have a few minutes to have coffee and chat with me. I have something to ask you. It's important."

Melanie had pulled on a short teal blue Spandex T-shirt and an Indian-print pleated skirt, one of those seventies styles that had begun making a comeback as soon as, at Rebecca's insistence, I had given all mine away. Melanie then slipped her feet into sandals and grabbed a large backpack suspended from a nearby chair. Before leaving, she stashed the bag of shoes in a locker and carefully turned the dial on the combination lock.

"Well, come with us. It only takes a few minutes. Then we can have a cup of coffee or whatever," said Tiffany. Her smile made it clear that this invitation was genuine. Melanie did not look enthusiastic but she did not protest either. So the three of us left the club and walked a block and a half east on Fourteenth Street to a large salon called Waxworks and More.

CHAPTER 22

CRUSADING LOCAL CLERGYMAN ATTENDS NATIONAL CONFERENCE ON MORALS

Carrington Chosen As Delegate to American Association of Lay Clergy

Will Carrington, charismatic leader of the Brethren of Believers Church in River Falls, has been chosen to represent area lay ministers at the American Association of Lay Clergy's annual conference in New York City. In spite of the withdrawal of a few delegates unwilling to travel to Manhattan, the conference will take place as scheduled. In addition to participating on a panel entitled "Family, Fidelity, and Faith," Brother Carrington will also present a paper on the successful premarital counseling program he initiated at Brethren of Believers called "Talk Now, Pray Later." The three-day conference will be hosted by the Best Western Hotel at . . .

This article was among the printouts of the material Illuminada found on Will Carrington that she had delivered to me later. The most noteworthy thing about the article was the photo of Carrington that accompanied it. He had smiled for the camera and his slicked-back hair gleamed even in the grainy black and white of a newspaper head shot. The handwritten note Illuminada had scrawled on a Post-it she stuck on the photo said only, *Bel, FYI, here's another photo to take to NY.* Tiffany and Melanie and I followed a tired-looking older woman with a name tag reading GERTA affixed to her three-quarter-length white jacket. Gerta led us past the reception desk and into the bowels of the bustling salon. I reached into my purse and brushed the envelope containing both photos with my fingertips to make sure I still had them.

Our guide pushed aside a curtain and we entered a large room that looked remarkably like a hospital's acute-care unit. There were gurney-like tables covered with white sheets. An overhead rod for a pastel curtain ringed each table. Some curtains were drawn around occupants, and others were open awaiting them.

The woman led us to two empty tables side by side. Before she drew the curtains, she looked me up and down and grunted, "You want?" For a moment I actually wavered. Maybe I should have a bikini wax. Maybe it would be rejuvenating. Then I realized that the last time I'd worn a bikini had been on my honeymoon with Lenny, my first husband. Besides, removing body hair had always been something I'd been ambivalent about, my furry inner feminist saying no and my silky-legged inner conformist saying yes. While I was reviewing this debate, my fingers closed over the envelope of photos, and I recalled the purpose of my visit. I shook my head but stayed put while Gerta drew the curtains around both tables, but left open the ones between the tables. "Okay?" she asked. The three of us nodded in unison.

In the time it had taken to establish the fact that I was not a customer, Melanie and Tiffany had stripped down to thongs and reclined, corpselike, each on her own table. The woman set to work at once, dusting down first Melanie and then Tiffany with a talcum that looked for all the world like confectioner's sugar, starkly white against their evenly tanned limbs. My nose instantly identified it as nothing more exotic than baby powder. Then Gerta dipped what looked like a popsicle stick into a small pot full of amber-colored wax. Next, wielding her gooey wand with the certainty of a true artiste, she smeared the warm wax generously over Melanie's thighs at the edges of her thong, covering each and every black hair that had dared to show itself. Satisfied that Melanie had been basted to a turn, she then pressed

232

a strip of white muslin over the wax, and suddenly, and quite forcibly, grabbed an end of this fabric and yanked off the whole schmear. My thighs quivered in empathy, but Melanie endured this assault in stoic silence. Peering closely at her work, Gerta pulled a tweezer out of her jacket pocket and used it to pluck a few recalcitrant hairs that had resisted her earlier efforts. Satisfied that Melanie's thighs were now completely hairless, she swabbed them down with a cotton ball immersed in a liquid my trusty nose recognized as baby oil. A summary grunt signaled to Melanie that she was free to dress. Now Gerta directed her ministrations to Tiffany.

While Gerta was preoccuppied with removing every wayward hair from Tiffany's thighs, I said quietly and without preamble to Melanie, "Would you mind taking a look at a couple of photos for me? I'd like to know if you recognize either of them." She hesitated for a split second and then nodded just before pulling her skirt on over her head. I had the photos ready and showed her the one of Nelson first.

Melanie answered right away, her voice low and matter-of-fact. "Yeah. He used to come around a lot when Eunice was here. Almost like a regular. I've only seen him once or twice since. She mentioned him a couple of times. Said he worked with her. She thought he was kind of a hypocrite, coming here the way he did and then giving her a hard time about dancing. It's very unusual for dudes we know to show up here. You know him too?" I was unprepared for Melanie's question.

"Actually, I do. I worked with Eunice as well, so he's a colleague of mine too. But tell me, what about this one?" I didn't want to give Melanie of the icy smile too much information, so I showed her Will's photo before she had a chance to ask me anything else. "Does this guy look familiar?"

Melanie pulled the photo closer and looked at it carefully. "No. I've never seen him here. But, remember I'm not here twenty-four/ seven. He could have come during somebody else's shift. Or I could have just missed him. A lot of times I just zone out. But Daphne might be able to ID him. She logs really long hours on the job because her son has to have special tutors." Melanie's muted monotone softened for a moment. "And Daphne eyeballs everybody who walks into the place when she's here. You should run these by Daphne." I hadn't mentioned the reason for my curiosity, but I sensed that Melanie realized I was trying to find out who killed Eunice and was glad. Maybe she wasn't personality plus, but maybe, just maybe, we were on the same side.

Over tea and sushi at a surprisingly good pan-Asian eatery two doors down from the

Waxworks, Tiffany said, "What were those pictures you were showing Melanie? Do I get to see them too?"

Quietly I said, "Yes. While the police are so preoccupied, I'm trying to figure out who might have killed Eunice. I've got some photos of possible suspects." Melanie nodded in silent acknowledgment of what she had assumed all along. Without saying anything further or waiting for a response, I showed Tiffany both photos. She too recognized Nelson. "He was one of Eunice's regulars, a new one. Now that she's gone, he only shows up maybe once a week. But I don't recognize this one," she said, pointing to Will's smiling face. "But you gotta show them both to Daphne. Not only because she's here more than God, but because she ought to know to keep an eye out for them," said Tiffany, echoing Melanie's advice. "After all, if you think maybe a customer killed Eunice, well . . . we all gotta be careful." Tiffany sighed, her chopsticks suspended over her tray, as she spoke. "It's like poor Eunice always said, 'We dancers should stick together.' " She thumped on the table with her free hand to emphasize her point.

"We can go back and run these by Daphne tonight if you want," she said. "The cops have been around here once, that's all, so far as I know. They're so busy what with the terrorists, the crazy traffic tie-ups downtown, and this anthrax crap that one dead dancer is just not going to get much of their attention right now." Tiffany shrugged and sighed again. "It's bad enough that the club was closed for most of September, but now that we've finally reopened, somebody stabs one of our dancers, and the cops like totally blow it off. Like she didn't matter at all. If she'd been a cop . . ." Tiffany's normally warm voice had become nasal and her words were coming in spurts. I wondered if she was fighting back tears.

"Yes, I know. The New Jersey police haven't been much more attentive either," I said. "That's why I thought I'd just try to do a little checking on my own. If I come up with any good leads, I could steer them in the right direction."

"You go, girl," said Melanie, flashing a warm smile for the first time since we'd met. The ice queen had melted. "How can we help?"

"Do you think there's anybody here who had it in for Eunice? Didn't like her? Was jealous of her? Argued with her?" I asked, picking up my California roll with my fingers and struggling to bite through the seaweed wrap without making too much of a mess. I envied my companions' facility with chopsticks. Both Tiffany and Melanie were eating daintily and with apparent gusto while I was trying not to dribble rice and avocado.

Tiffany and Melanie exchanged glances and then Tiffany said, "The only person Eunice really got to was Queenie."

"Queenie couldn't stand the way Eunice stood up to her, baited her. Eunice was such a big draw here that she could get away with it. Mike would never get rid of Eunice, but Queenie hated the way Eunice kept on pushing for sick days and health benefits. Eunice didn't think we should have to pay a weekly stage fee to dance either," said Melanie. "My husband says Eunice was right. He thinks we're really exploited," she added.

"Let's face it. What really got Queenie was the fact that everybody else here slips her a little something extra besides the stage fee once in a while to get a schedule change or an extra set or something. But not Eunice. She just gave Queenie a sheet of paper saying when she was available to dance and gave a copy to Mike. Queenie was really honked," recalled Tiffany.

"That's right," said Melanie. "Eunice wouldn't play Queenie's little game, and she let everybody know it. Queenie was scared we'd all do the same thing, but we didn't. The rest of us have kids and college loans and other bills or whatever." Now it was her turn to sigh. "Queenie can make your life miserable just by scheduling you when she knows you can't get a sitter or when you have a class or go to your day job." Now it

237

was my turn to sigh as I recalled the fact that in the parallel universe of academic life, the department chair, the one who schedules classes, also exerts power over faculty and students alike far out of proportion to his or her position. And while we didn't try to bribe Harold with money to honor our requests for particular days and courses, who among my colleagues has not offered to chair a particularly odious committee in return for a three-day schedule?

"Would Queenie kill Eunice?" I asked.

Again Tiffany and Melanie exchanged glances, then shook their heads almost in unison. "A long time ago when she was married, Queenie took in four foster kids. Now they're older and she's putting three of them through college," Melanie explained.

"You mean we're putting three of them through college," said Tiffany with a laugh. "Every dollar she skims off us goes to pay tuition for one of those kids. That's why she was so pissed off at Eunice. Eunice didn't care to contribute to Queenie's scholarship fund. Hey, we've got to get back soon. What do you say we take you to talk to Daphne?"

Although I wasn't sure I followed their reasoning, I agreed to return with Melanie and Tiffany to the Big Apple Peel to play show-and-tell with Daphne. If I wanted to, I could always catch up with Queenie some other time.

CHAPTER 23

To: Bbarrett@circle.com
From: Mbarrett@hotmail.com
Re: Give me a break
Date: 11/09/01 08:09:46

Yo, Ma Bel,

So what's going on? Aveda says Sol called to say we're all having Thanksgiving at Alexis's house. But Grandma Sadie says we're still going to Rebecca and Keith's. Man, is our family being especially dysfunctional just 'cause I'm bringing my girlfriend to meet them for the first time or is this just the way we always are and I forgot? If we aren't going to all be together at Rebecca's, I might as well try to change the plane tickets Grandma Sadie sent and bring Aveda to spend the holiday weekend at Dad's house. He and Cissie invited us a long time ago, and even though I'll miss your scalloped oysters and Cissie is a vegan now, at least she and Dad are both on the same page of their heinous menu.

Love anyway,
Mark

I didn't know whether to laugh or cry at Mark's e-mail. His blatant guilt-inducing manipulation and totally narcissistic concern about *his* girl and *his* plane tickets, and *his* holiday meal would have been laughable if they hadn't been reminders of Sol's genuine and apparently worsening distress. And reading between the lines, I knew that Mark's sarcasm signaled that, in reality, he was worried about us. I was worried too. But Sol was having dinner with Marlene that evening, a good sign I thought. Meanwhile I didn't have time to dwell on Mark's message and put off answering it for a day or two. Perhaps by then I'd have good news to convey.

But I also wanted to talk to Andrea Goodson, and I wanted to do it soon. To that end I called Linda Markey and left word that I would be coming to the Gotham Treatment Center at three that afternoon to see Andrea about an urgent family matter. I requested that Ms. Markey leave a visitor's pass for me with the receptionist as well as a phone message confirming that she had done so. My last class ended at two, and I had no conferences scheduled for the rest of the day. I resolved to skip a meeting of the committee assigned to review and rewrite RECC's mission statement for the fourth time after having determined that the agenda consisted of rereading the three earlier drafts.

I left RECC after class and caught the

PATH train to Fourteenth Street right away. That afternoon, the streets of the Village appeared eerily empty of everyone but those who lived or worked there, so once again it was too easy to get a cab. I made it to the Gotham Center at exactly three. This time Andrea stood just inside the reception area, obviously waiting for me. She wore jeans, a blue work shirt, and her green clogs. Her shirt sleeves were rolled up, and when she moved her arms, I could see scars circling not one but both wrists. Her dark hair was tied back, and behind her glasses her eyes were still. Today her resemblance to Eunice seemed even more pronounced than it had been on the evening of our first meeting. Her entire affect was more subdued, and I wondered if she were medicated or depressed, or both. It occurred to me that Andrea might appreciate having the things she had left at Eunice's. I'd have to see about getting them to her sometime.

"Hey, Professor," Andrea said before the receptionist had even checked my ID and given me my visitor's pass. I took off my coat and pinned the name tag to my jumper.

"Hi, Andrea, good to see you. You look kind of down," I said.

"I'm okay, I guess," she answered, her voice wavering a little. We took a few steps away from the receptionist's station. "You want to come to the all-purpose room again?

241

A few residents may be in there playing cards or whatnot, but it's really the only place we can go."

"The all-purpose room sounds fine," I said, touched by her effort to play hostess in this grim place.

Except for a few women sitting in one corner watching a Spanish soap opera on a small wall-mounted television set, we had the room to ourselves. Without discussion, we both headed for the far corner where the sounds from the TV were only a high-pitched background babble. Once again we sat opposite each other, and once again, Andrea lit a cigarette. "Andrea, you know the cops here and in New Jersey are pretty busy right now, right?"

"Yeah," she said. "But I'm still glad I'm not out there using and turning tricks anymore. I want to stay clean and try to get some schooling like Eunie wanted me to, you know?"

"I'm glad to hear that," I said, almost amused that she still had a junkie's-eye-view of the preoccupations of the police. The fact that the NYPD might have other more global concerns now than apprehending hookers and heroin users had not really registered with her. I would have to lead her to where I wanted her to go in this conversation. "What I mean is that because of what happened at the World Trade Center, the police are too busy to pay much attention right now to finding out who killed your sister, so I'm doing a little poking around myself."

Andrea nodded solemnly. Then she asked, "You mean like a detective?" There was disbelief in her voice, but also intrigue in her brightening eyes. "You don't look like a detective," she said taking in my black corduroy jumper, burgundy silk turtleneck, fly-away frizzy hair, and the reading glasses suspended from a chain around my neck. "I mean you look so, oh, you know, so like a professor," she sputtered, obviously trying to avoid hurting my feelings. She rubbed first one magenta-ringed wrist and then the other. I wondered if they still hurt.

"Well, I am a professor, but that's neither here nor there. Listen, Andrea. I'm very upset about Eunice's death, and I want to make sure that whoever killed her is apprehended and punished." Andrea's expression didn't change when I said this, so I went on. "Right now the police are so desperate to close this case that they are accusing a girl I know who is no more capable of having killed Eunice than you are." There was still not even a flicker in response to this statement in Andrea's features or body language. That she might be a suspect hadn't even occurred to her. "In fact, when the cops figure out that Eunice had a sister and find you, they might accuse you too," I said in what I hoped was a menacing tone. Andrea looked stricken, as if I'd smacked her.

"Well, I did kill her in a way. I told you. If I hadn't given Will Carrington the name of that club, he'd never have found her, you know?" She spoke sadly now as if resigned to the grim role she had written for herself in the tragedy of her sister's death.

"Andrea, do you have an alibi for the night of October 20, the night Eunice was killed? Where were you that night at about midnight?" I asked.

"I was across the street from the Big Apple Peel waiting for Eunie to come out. That's the night I went to meet her. I thought she got out at about one a.m., you know, but she didn't show. I told you."

"Are you sure?" I persisted. Andrea nodded, stubbing out her cigarette. With her hands free, she resumed rubbing her wrists, first one and then the other.

"So how do you know Will Carrington went there and killed her? What makes you so certain?" I could have added that junky hookers were not always considered reliable sources of information, but I refrained.

But Andrea understood the implication of what I had left unsaid. When she spoke, her voice had an insistent edge. "I saw him. He waited at the door, and when she came out, they . . ."

"So she did come out," I said, annoyed

with Andrea for lying and trying to figure out why she'd bothered. No matter how she told the story, she herself had no alibi for that night. On the contrary, she admitted to having been at the club and to having sent the postcard. So why didn't I believe that Andrea had killed her sister?

Andrea looked up at me with the round eyes of a child caught in a fib. "Yes, okay, okay. She came out. And she saw Will. She didn't recognize him, you know? I could tell because when he reached to take her arm, she started to go back inside, like he was some kind of stalker or something. But then he must have said who he was because all of a sudden she turned around and looked at him and let out this big yell, and they hugged and walked away together. It was like they were having their own personal high school reunion. She never even looked for me. She just blew me off for that no-good whoring hypocrite." As I sat there, she caressed each wrist in turn.

Suddenly I understood. Andrea had preferred to say that Eunice had not left work rather than acknowledging that her long-suffering sister had finally rejected her. Eunice had been like a mother to her, and, like a child, Andrea was jealous of anybody who seemed to displace her in Eunice's heart, even Will Carrington. Was that why Andrea was so eager to incriminate him? "Your postcard was delivered to Eunice's apartment after her death. The mail has been a little slow lately," I said softly. "The post office has been disrupted by the anthrax scare."

As Andrea digested the implications of these facts, I pressed her. "You followed them, of course." It was a guess, but I knew that that night Andrea had been desperate. She could not return to the abusive Enrique. A city shelter was a last resort. Maybe she had figured that if she waited to show herself until Eunice and Will had finished their reunion, Eunice would take pity on her, let her crash at her place for a few days, and help her get into a rehab program.

"You really are a detective," said Andrea, surprise lifting her head and brightening her eyes for a second time. "Yes, I followed them to the PATH station. I went downstairs after them and even paid so I could get onto the platform. I stayed behind in the crowd, so she wouldn't see me. Carrington paid too, so I figured he was going home with her. She got on the train, waving to somebody who was already on, but Carrington stayed on the platform. She and Carrington were both talking and joking. Then just as the last passengers were getting on the train, she leaned over and gave Carrington a big kiss, like in those old war movies on TV, you know?"

"So did you get on the train that night?" I

asked, pretty sure of what the answer would be.

"Nope. I was just standing there watching, and before I pulled myself together, the doors closed and the train pulled out. But Will got on." Andrea reported, looking up to see how I reacted to this news. Her hands lay quietly in her lap.

"Will got on the train? I thought you just said Eunice kissed him good-bye?" Had drug use messed up Andrea's mind? Or was her whole story just that, a story? And had she forgotten the thread of her own narrative?

Andrea lit another cigarette, took a deep drag, and exhaled it slowly. Her words were clearly audible through the resulting cloud of smoke. "I saw him jump on right before the doors closed. He practically knocked over whoever she was talking to. I couldn't see that dude's face, but he must have been surprised. Eunie was laughing." With great effort, I kept still. Then she said, "That's when I finally realized I couldn't count on Eunie. I figured this time she'd really given up on me, you know? I needed to take care of myself." At the recollection of this overdue epiphany, Andrea's chin jutted out and her back straightened. Once again her resemblance to Eunice was unmistakable. "I went to a diner where I'm friends with one of the waitresses, Rena. She's a little older, you know? Rena let me sit there until morning." If Andrea noticed me twisting my mouth to avoid smiling at how she had taken care of herself by seeking out yet another mother figure, she gave no sign. "She gave me a free breakfast, and let me use her cell to call one of those hotlines for abused women, you know? So to make a long story short, finally they sent me here."

I had arranged to have dinner with Betty and Illuminada at Satay, a Malaysian place in Hoboken where I figured we could process whatever I gleaned from Tiffany, Melanie, and Andrea. I was glad because by the time I had left Andrea at the end of the afternoon, I was more bewildered than ever. I was the last to arrive at the restaurant. My pleasure at being reunited with my friends and enjoying a good meal was considerably diminished when I remembered that Satay does not have a liquor license. Seeing my stricken face and reading my mind, Betty said, "Not to worry, girlfriend. I brought some vino."

"*Chiquita,* you look like you really need a glass of something right away." As Illuminada spoke, Betty pulled a bottle of Australian Chardonnay out of her tote bag with the flourish of a magician pulling a rabbit out of a hat. She waved the bottle at a passing waiter who was carrying a full tray of food to another table. Nodding to acknowledge her signal, he dispensed the plates on his tray and returned with a corkscrew and three wineglasses. For once I was grateful for Betty's peremptory way with servers. She got results.

As soon as he had filled each of our glasses and taken our order for appetizers, I began to speak. "You would not believe how confused I am. How the hell am I going to get to talk to Will Carrington? I mean he lives in upstate New York. And yet, he's the most likely suspect in a way. But no one I talked to saw him at the club."

"And here's to you too," said Betty, effectively cutting me off as she raised her glass. We usually toasted peace or health or some other desirable abstraction before drinking. I could see that Betty would brook no break with tradition. Still grateful that she'd provided the wine, I swallowed my words, and we raised our glasses to the increasingly unlikely prospect of world peace.

"Bel, let's order our entrees before you tell us what you found out. That way we don't have to interrupt you again," said Betty, still micromanaging the meal and the conversation.

As the wine hit my insides, I realized that my day had been lunchless. Since I consider missing a meal potentially life threatening, I agreed to order before continuing even though I was very eager to unload my findings on Betty and Illuminada. While I waited for our waiter to return and waited to talk,

249

dinner began to feel like an exercise in the dreaded deferred gratification. Thank goodness I had a glass of wine to sip during this high-stress interval. Just as I was beginning to lose patience, our waiter materialized bearing our chicken satays.

After he had recorded our entree orders, Illuminada said, "So, *chiquita,* what did you learn?" Brandishing her satay like a mini wand, she pointed at me and said, "Tell all." I did. It took over half an hour for me to rehash the meeting with Melanie and Tiffany and the later one with Daphne. "So let me get this straight," said Illuminada, holding her wineglass for Betty to refill. "Two dancers and the woman who works the cash register did not recognize Will Carrington. But all three recognized Nelson Vandergast. And you're all worked up over questioning Carrington?"

"Yes. Daphne not only recognized Nelson, but she said she'd had several conversations with him because he asked to leave brochures for Soprano Safari Tours at the club's cash register. Nelson figured that since the Big Apple Peel attracts a lot of tourists, some of them might be Soprano fans and might want to take his tour. Daphne was the liaison between Nelson and Mike, the owner, because Mike was never around when Nelson came. So Daphne asked Mike, and Mike cut Nelson a deal. For a monthly fee, Nelson can leave his brochures at the register," I said. "Apparently Nelson's disapproval of stripping doesn't prevent him from advertising at a strip club or visiting one himself," I added, disdain sharpening my diction.

"And it may not have prevented him from killing a stripper either," said Betty. "Anyway, you've established that Nelson Vandergast has visited the club." She helped herself to another serving of shrimp with mango sauce and passed the platter.

"*Chiquita,* we already knew that because Bel saw him there the night we all went, remember?" said Illuminada, her chopsticks poised over her plate.

"Right," said Betty, smacking her head with her hand. "Senior half hour. Sorry. Well, what's with this other guy? This Carrington dude? Why are you so hot to talk to him, Bel?"

We had polished off the last vestige of shrimp with mango sauce and chicken with bitter melon by the time I had finished relating that afternoon's conversation with Andrea. The Chardonnay bottle was empty. Illuminada was leaning forward, one hand propping up her chin and the other drumming on the table. A few seconds after I stopped speaking, she sat back and said, "I still think Andrea is pushing your sympathy button. I still think she fabricated this story of Eunice's long-lost love coming to New

251

York and murdering her in a decade-old fit of jealousy and moral outrage. *But,* we have to check it out." She sounded resigned as she reminded us of her own insistence on checking out all leads, even the most unlikely.

"I know that. I just don't have time to go to upstate New York and talk to him," I said.

"Remember when we had to get that dude back from Arizona?" Betty asked, referring to a witness to a murder we'd been involved with sometime before. "You lured him back here for a phony job interview, remember? Well, I could call this Carrington and threaten to leak it to his local newspaper that he was picking up hookers in New York while he was here. I bet his congregation would just love that," she said, looking very pleased with herself.

It was a brilliant idea, easy, fast, cheap, and surefire. "Betty, for the second time tonight, I want to throw my arms around you," I said, putting down my teacup lest in my excitement I slop tea all over. "He'll come and then we can grill him and at least find out if he was really there or has an alibi. Let's figure out what you're going to say."

"Right, we'll keep the dialog short and sweet. You can call him from the ladies room here. It's pretty quiet," said Illuminada. "I've got his number somewhere."

By the time we left the Satay we had a

date to meet a very nervous Will Carrington
at 7:30 the following night at the Mrs. Fields
cookie shop in the Port Authority Bus Terminal in New York.

CHAPTER 24

To: Bbarrett@circle.com
From: Ldonovan@juno.com
Re: Renovationblues
Date: 11/10/01 14:38:29

Dear Down and Dirty in Hoboken,

Well, I can't say I blame you for bitching about your renovation. What with the dust and delays, it sounds nightmarish. But at least you and your partner have a solid relationship, and you have a contractor you can trust. When Jerry and I decided to renovate our bathroom, who knew it would mean the end of our marriage?

We hired Neil, the contractor who gave the lowest estimate, after his references swore he was God's gift to home improvement. And he was. In fact, he was so competent that even before he finished tiling our bathroom, we recommended him to Jerry's daughter, Elyse, and her husband, who wanted to add a wing to their McMansion.

Now I should mention that Elyse is just

like her mother, a manipulative gold digger who lives to shop and play golf. She has never accepted Jerry's remarriage and tried her best to prevent it. She is barely civil to me. She once handed me a Weight Watchers' brochure in front of a client of mine. Another time she told a neighbor her father had married beneath him. But in the ten years I've been Jerry's wife, I've never said a negative word to him about Elyse because the miserable bitch is his only child and he dotes on her. A shrink I saw about this gave me what seemed like good advice at the time. Who knew? She said I should keep a diary and describe every bitchy thing Elyse said or did to me and how I felt about it. I usually kept this diary in a drawer in my night table.

One day the doorbell rang while I was writing, and I left the damn diary out and forgot about it. While I was at work, Neil saw it and read it. Can you imagine? Just wait. It gets better. The sneaky little bastard actually tried to blackmail me! Can you imagine? He took the diary and told me that unless I gave him five thousand dollars, he would show Elyse what I'd written about her. Of course, I said nothing doing. He showed it to Elyse. She flipped out and showed it to Jerry, who closed ranks with his daughter and moved out, leaving me with an empty bathroom and an empty bed. I've had Neil charged with theft and extortion, but Elyse got him a clever lawyer, and I don't think he'll do jail time. So count your blessings that renovation hasn't wrecked your romance.

Lonely in White Plains

This was the saddest e-mail I had gotten in response to my plea for support, but I tried not to focus on the writer's lurid account of blackmail and broken families after we got to the Port Authority. I was too keyed up at the prospect of confronting Will Carrington. Illuminada stood near the front of the candy shop immediately adjacent to Mrs. Fields'. As she eyed the colorful display of hard candies, she could see Betty, who stood by the railing opposite the stores, and she could see me, ogling the selection of warm cookies in the display case. Of course, we could see her too, and it was comforting to know that Illuminada's trim pants leg concealed a small ankle holster and gun and that she had another revolver in her Coach bag. Her right hand was poised on the lip of her purse.

We had arrived at 7:15, but when there was no sign of Will Carrington by 8:00, Betty phoned the bus company to see if the bus he'd said he was taking had arrived. It had. The next one wasn't due until 8:30. We waited.

Betty called Carrington at the number she had used the previous evening and his machine answered. "I know that dude was going to show here," she said, frustration amplifying her voice. "When I told him that the working girl he'd tried to hook up with would testify to his local paper if he didn't get his two-timing double-standard butt in here tonight, he was already running to buy his bus ticket." By ten o'clock two more buses had arrived without Carrington. In the meantime, Betty and I had each eaten two full-sized chocolate chunk cookies and were contemplating a third.

Then suddenly, inspired, perhaps, by the e-mail account of blackmail in White Plains that was still ruffling the fringes of my consciousness, I had a grim thought. "What if he killed himself?" I speculated aloud. "What if he felt guilty and got scared that we were going to blackmail him? What if he doesn't have the money to pay us off, so he just killed himself?" We were on the bus home by this time, whizzing through the nearly empty Lincoln Tunnel near the back of a nearly empty bus.

Betty looked stricken. "Lord, I didn't mean to scare him to death. I just wanted to make sure he showed up. Geez," she said, the sound coming out in a kind of moan. The specter of suicide was especially unsettling to her Catholic sensibility.

"Relax, *chiquita*," said Illuminada from across the aisle. "You're powerful, but you're not that powerful. And even if he did kill himself, it's his doing, not yours. He tried to pick up a hooker while he was at a conference for *lay* clergy," she said archly and with unmistakable emphasis on the word "lay." "Give me a break. But, Bel might still be onto something. He might have killed himself if he thought he was going to be exposed as Eunice's murderer. Or, who knows? He might have killed himself because he killed her in a fit of passion. When we get out of this tunnel, I'm going to call the local cops up there and see if they've found any bodies lately."

Illuminada was as good as her word. As soon as the bus emerged from the tunnel, she punched in a number on her cell and was soon talking to the police dispatcher in Carrington's upstate hometown. "Private Investigator Guttierez here. I'm looking for someone who may have disappeared in your neck of the woods in the last twenty-four hours. Any suicides? Missing persons? Anything?" She paused. "Yes, I'll hold." She shrugged and then spoke again. "Yes, hello, Chief Thorne. Yes, I run a New Jersey-based PI firm. Yes, please check the website. www.IguttierezPI.com. I'll hold, but my question is very general. Yes, I'll wait." If Chief Thorne had had even the faintest idea of how Illuminada felt about waiting for anything, he'd have thought twice about keeping her on hold. As it was, she didn't have to wait long. In a moment she was speaking again. "Yes, Chief Thorne, can you tell me if there have been any disappearances or perhaps a suicide up your way in the past twenty-four hours? No suicides. I see. Oh, I see. I see. *Dios mío,* I see. Thank you very much. No, I can't say, Chief, but thanks again."

In the glow of the streetlights that illuminated the interior of the bus, I could see that Illuminada's brow was practically pleated in consternation as she pushed the button that turned off her cell. "They haven't had any disappearances or suicides, but William Carrington was found stabbed to death in an alley behind the Greyhound bus terminal early this morning. They have no clue who did it. According to Chief Thorne, Carrington, quote, didn't have an enemy in the world, unquote."

Even though it was late, we needed to process this astounding information and explore its implications, if any, for our investigation of Eunice's murder. Silently we got off the bus at the Malibu Diner, a venerable and glitzy eaterie at the northern end of Hoboken. We took a corner table and tried to think of something we could order to justify our presence there. "*Dios mío,* I didn't have supper. I'll have a Swiss cheese omelet and an English muffin," said Illuminada. Betty and I ordered decaf teas to wash down the cookies we'd enjoyed earlier.

"Illuminada, will you get your buddy Chief Thorne to send an autopsy report on Carrington?" I asked. It wasn't so much that I thought that this document would shed light on Eunice's murder as that the request for an autopsy seemed somehow an appropriate next move. Having made it, I sat there silent, totally at a loss as to the move to make after that. Betty sipped her tea. Illuminada was applying a minuscule dab of butter to her English muffin. Finally I spoke. "Let's brainstorm why somebody would have wanted Carrington dead, okay?" I said, stifling a yawn. I had an early class the next morning and was beginning to feel the effects of the long day I'd put in. I hoped the tea would kick in soon.

"Try to stay awake, Bel," said Betty getting out her Palm Pilot so she could take notes. "Well, there's always his wife. Maybe this wasn't the first time he'd strayed and she was fed up." Betty typed as she spoke.

"Maybe he was abusive too," said Illuminada whose grim view of American family life never ceased to amaze me. "Or, *chiquitas,* maybe Eunice's sister, Andrea, followed him back upstate and iced him. After all, Bel thinks little orphan Andrea considered him a rival for Eunice's affection."

"She'd never do that," I said quickly. "Besides, Andrea's in the Gotham Treatment Center, remember? She has an airtight alibi for last night." Now it was Illuminada's turn to look chagrined and say, "Of course. Sorry, senior half hour."

"Listen, girlfriends, let's look at the big picture," said Betty. "Maybe he had an enemy upstate, someone we know nothing about. After all, he doesn't sound like a very nice man. Maybe there's a jealous husband up there who wanted him dead or a rival minister or a betrayed lover for that matter." Her voice was low now and husky from fatigue.

"I need to pack it in for tonight," I said. "Even the tea isn't jump-starting me. I'm beat. But let's focus on who might have wanted *both* Eunice Goodson and Will Carrington dead. After all, they both come from the same town . . ."

"Are you suggesting that this is one of those back-to-the-future kind of killings with its roots in their high school romance?" asked Betty.

"Are you thinking we should be looking through their yearbook trying to figure out who didn't get asked to the prom and carried a grudge for ten years and . . ." said Illuminada, getting out a credit card.

"All I'm saying is we need to at least think

about who might have wanted them both dead," I repeated. "I know you think Nelson killed Eunice," I said to Betty. "And I know you think Andrea killed her," I said to Illuminada. "But frankly, at this point I don't have a clue who the hell killed the poor woman. Not a clue."

CHAPTER 25

Soprano Safari, Inc.

Tour Soprano country on a comfortable bus with Jersey born and bred Soprano scholar Professor Nelson Vandergast as your guide. A member of the faculty of River Edge Community College, Professor Vandergast offers an informed and insightful back-story on each of the following sites: Big Pussy's Auto Body Shop, Satriale's Pork Store, Satin Dolls (the Bada Bing Club), the Paterson Falls, and Tony's social club. Professor Vandergast will also answer questions inspired by a video presentation of the suburban home of Victor and Patti Recchia that is the model for Tony and Carmela's dream McMansion (soon to be featured in *Architectural Digest*). Members of the safari will visit the notorious New Jersey Meadowlands, final resting place of several of Tony Soprano's less fortunate business associates. Espresso and cannoli served on all safaris. Dinner tours and group rates available. For safari schedule, ticket prices, and reservations, call 555 452-9107 or visit www.sopranosafari.com.

Group rates available. Special rates for school groups.

The ad copy in the Soprano Safaris leaflet differed from that on their web page primarily in that it was slightly more academic in tone. Instead of featuring a headshot of Nelson on the front, the double-sided placard boasted a large portrait of James Gandolfini on the front, and only a postage-stamp-sized one of Nelson on the back. Practicing the zeal for marketing he no doubt preached to his students, Nelson Vandergast had scrawled his latest request for a conference on the bottom of this red-and-black-edged flyer and left it in my mailbox. Apparently he entertained the fantasy that I might someday take a Soprano safari myself. Very curious as to what he might want to see me about, I had e-mailed Nelson that I would meet with him during my morning office hours.

The night before had been a restless one for me. My sleep had been repeatedly interrupted by disturbing dreams. One featured the spacious Soprano kitchen ravaged by renovation. In it a hapless workman who looked a lot like Ed knelt before Tony, pleading for his life. There was another dream in which I was forcibly subjected to a bikini wax on the platform of the Hoboken PATH station at rush hour while someone waved at me from a departing train. In yet another, Ronni

Illysario threatened to blackmail me. She said if I didn't find Eunice's killer, she would tell everyone at RECC and everyone in our neighborhood that Sol had cracked up and that we were moving to the sticks. Small wonder that when I awoke, I was sweating and anxious.

Sol was already downstairs by the time I showered and dressed. When I opened the bedroom door and the familiar strains of "Nearer My God to Thee" wafted up the stairs, disbelief dueled with delight in my tired brain. Was it possible? Was Ed back from jury duty? "Ed!" I called. "Sol! Is Ed really back? For good?"

"None other, Professor," said Ed, emerging from the back of the house with Sol, who was smiling, something he rarely did anymore. "I was tellin' Sol, they let us out after only three days. It was a hit-and-run with witnesses, an open-and-shut case," he said, flashing his familiar grin. "So I'm just gonna get crackin' on these windows and then finish up these cabinets and you'll have the prettiest kitchen this side of anywhere." It was amazing how fast Ed's reappearance altered my mood and energized me. After giving him a bear hug, I practically skipped around the house gathering my things.

That was why I didn't notice one of Ed's toolboxes open on the floor next to the stack of windows before I tripped over it. Grabbing on to the banister behind me, I saved myself from a nasty fall, but drawings, screws, nails, washers, and other little metal gizmos were now part of the mosaic of dust and shavings on our floor. "Oh, Ed, I'm sorry," I said, bending to gather them, shake them off, and replace them in the metal box along with the sketches, receipts, and some other papers that had also fallen out.

"No problem. I'm the one who should be sorry. I shouldn't have left my gear there. Sol just got me goin' on somethin', and I forgot about it. You sure you're okay?" Concern lowered Ed's normally hearty voice.

"I'm fine. I'm just glad you're on the job again, that's all," I said, resisting the impulse to rub my ankle where it had hit the metal box. Soon the sound of the sander drowned out the hymns, but for once the noise didn't bother me, and when I left for work I found myself humming. Even Sol was smiling now that Ed was back.

I stopped in the still-dark English Department office to pick up my mail and to use the microwave to nuke water for tea. As I stood waiting for the water to heat, I noted an OUT OF ORDER sign taped to the Xerox machine. This all-too-familiar announcement meant that I would have to scurry around the building begging secretaries of other departments to let me Xerox my handouts for the Faculty Development

Seminar on their machines. Or, failing that, I would have to try to persuade the RECC copy shop to Xerox them for me without having given the requisite advance notice in triplicate. Why was life so complicated?

The microwave beeped, the series of bleats shrill in the dim and empty office. I reached to press open the door. Suddenly a strong hand gripped my shoulder from behind. I started, nearly dropping my mail. A gruff male voice said, "Wait. Let me get that for you, Professor. You've got your hands full already." It was Nelson, and all at once I felt uneasy. What was he doing in the empty English Department office at that hour? Our appointment wasn't for another twenty minutes, and my office was at the other end of the hall. What was he up to here? Betty was convinced he'd murdered Eunice, and I had no proof that he hadn't. Suddenly I saw him as a person who might very well have wanted both Eunice and Will Carrington dead. What if he'd fallen for Eunice and she'd discouraged him? What if he'd hung out at the Big Apple Peel and seen her leave with Carrington? Why hadn't I thought of this last night? Damn. The building's one security guard was nowhere to be seen.

"Sorry, I didn't mean to scare you," Nelson said, removing my thermos of water from the microwave and handing it to me.

"What are you doing here?" I asked, anxiety reducing my voice to a low croak.

"The Xerox machine in the Business Department's broken, so I thought I'd come down here early, before the secretary shows up, and use this one. I know the code," he said, looking embarrassed. Even his embarrassment looked suspicious to me now. Before I could inquire as to how a member of the business faculty had come to know the code of the English Department Xerox machine, Nelson said, "Eunice got it and gave it to me, and I gave her ours." He frowned at the mention of the dead woman's name and then shrugged. "Well, we figured since the ones in our departments are always broken, we'd be able to come in early and use this one. We figured it would even out in the long run."

"Well, that'll teach you," I said. I was acutely conscious of the fact that I was bantering about copy machines with a possible killer. "I guess they're all broken today," I said, unable to change the subject.

"Who knew?" said Nelson shrugging his shoulders again. "The best laid plans . . ."

"Well, Nelson, why don't we go to my office and begin our conference a little early? We'll both need the extra time to try to find a working Xerox machine later on," I said, still unable to let the topic go. But I was eager to get out of the empty office and into the corridor where, by this time, students and faculty would be filtering in to their first classes of the day.

"It's a plan," said Nelson, pushing open the office door and holding it for me. Once out in the hall, I felt my fears and suspicions about Nelson dissipating. Even so, after we had settled ourselves in the two chairs in my office, I made a point of keeping the door ajar. I'd been trapped in the tiny cubicle with a man who had homicidal tendencies once too often to risk it again. I had a strictly open-door policy now.

"So, Nelson, what did you want to talk about with me?" I asked as soon as I had reclaimed my thermos and plopped a tea bag into it. "Is it about your project?" During the course of the semester, each seminar participant was required to complete a paper centered on changes in curriculum or pedagogy or both.

"No. Honestly, Professor, I haven't even started that." Perhaps because he saw my eyebrows go up, he hastily added, "Not to worry though. I know what I'm going to do my project on."

"Are you planning to tell me?" I asked, half in jest. Seminar participants were required to submit proposals for their projects for my approval.

"I'll have it outlined for you by next week, I swear. I just have to work out a few details," said Nelson. "I wanted to ask your opinion about something. You're my mentor. You see . . ."

"Go on," I said when his pause had lasted a few seconds.

"Okay. You remember I run Soprano Safaris, right?" He pointed to his T-shirt on which SOPRANO was written in blood red letters and SAFARIS in black ones. "I give tours of the sites on the Sopranos show. You saw my brochure, right?" Nelson had reached into his briefcase and was holding one of the leaflets in his hand.

"No, but I've seen your website. It's quite good," I answered, now really curious about where this was going. I sipped my tea and waited.

"Thanks, Professor. The brochures are quite similar. See." He handed me a leaflet. "What do you think about my giving these out to my students? A lot of them are really big Sopranos fans. Do you see anything wrong with that?" While he spoke, I glanced at the flyer.

"I'm glad you asked me, Nelson," I said, putting the flyer on my desk. "I have a pretty definite opinion on this subject."

"I mean none of them would *have* to go," he said, as if I hadn't spoken. "But I hate to deprive them of the chance of even knowing about the safaris either. That doesn't seem right. Besides, the tours make great holiday gifts. Whole families take them together. I

270

bet my students would love to know about them," said Nelson, gesturing toward the flyer on my desk. I sat with the fingertips of one hand against those of the other, making like the sounding board the young man clearly needed as a witness to the battle between his inner marketer and his role as educator.

"It's not like I would sell tour tickets in class or anything like that. I know that would be wrong." Nelson watched my face as he spoke. "At least I think it would," he said. "But, you know, lots of faculty members take students on field trips, and this is certainly related to their studies as business majors. I'm a role model for them." Noticing my mouth twist a little at this, he added quickly. "I'm an entrepreneur, and my students could go and see how my business works, what goes into it. It would be invaluable for them." Nelson's eyes gleamed at the prospect of sharing his entrepreneurial empire with his students — for a fee. "So what do you think?" he asked, this time actually waiting for me to reply.

"I agree that it could be helpful for your students to explore your business with you. But I think you should take them for free," I said.

Nelson's eyes widened, and he straightened in his chair. "For free? You must be kidding. Nobody goes on a Soprano Safari for free.

271

Even my mother had to pay." Indignation was making his words come out faster and louder. At any moment he would be sputtering. I suddenly pictured Nelson as a kid running a lemonade stand and charging his mother for that too.

"Yes, Nelson. For free. Otherwise you're pressuring your students to buy a product that you're selling, and that's not a fair use of the power inherent in your role as professor," I said, trying not to let impatience sharpen my tongue. "Some of your students will feel that they won't get a good grade unless they pay for a tour. It's called conflict of interest." Nelson looked blank, as if I were speaking Greek. I searched for an example, all the time wondering why I was teaching business ethics to a member of the RECC business faculty. "Do you know that if you wrote a textbook for a course you're teaching, you could require your own students to buy it, but in some states you'd also be mandated by law to give the royalties from all books purchased by your own students to charity?"

Nelson looked stunned. "No. You're kidding, right, Professor?"

"No, Nelson, I'm not kidding. You think about it and talk about it with other colleagues and see what they say. Meanwhile, I have a class to teach in a few minutes. I'll see you during seminar this afternoon and we can pursue this with the others."

It wasn't until he had been gone for a few minutes that I noticed the flyer still on my desk. I reached to sweep it into the circular file and then stopped. Maybe I would go sometime after all. Come to think of it, Sofia and Ma were rabid Soprano fans, and they would probably love a Soprano Safari. Score one for Nelson the marketer. I picked up the leaflet and put it in my purse.

I needn't have bothered. When I arrived home that afternoon, there was an identical red-and-black-edged flyer on the table at the door. "Get a load of that," said Sol, when he saw me eyeing it. "Somebody actually gives tours of Sopranos sites! I bet he makes a nice chunk of change too! What an amazing country this is!" he said. "Anybody with an idea . . ."

Sol looked a little hurt when I interrupted his ode to American capitalism. "Where did you get that? Did it come in the mail?"

"No. I spotted it on the floor when I was playing with Virginia Woolf. It's probably Ed's. He's a Sopranos nut. It must've fallen out of his toolbox when you knocked it over this morning," Sol answered. "I wonder if he took the tour."

Of course. Of course. I felt beads of sweat coalesce on my forehead. This piece of information Sol had just imparted so casually jarred loose some others and now they were all whirling around in my brain like clothes in a dryer. Putting my finger to my lips in a signal for Sol to be quiet, I walked over to the steps and sat down, for once ignoring the dust and wood shavings. I held my head in my hands. My head was literally spinning, the word that best describes what my brain does while it is synthesizing seemingly disparate facts into a pattern. Like a quilter who patches together discarded and motley scraps of fabric to form a geometric shape, I could sometimes organize what appeared to be random phenomena in such a way as to make sense out of them. This was a relatively new ability of mine, a special kind of wisdom that had arrived to grace my middle years.

Sol knew better than to interrupt this process. Only after I stood up, did he speak. "So tell me, love. What did you just figure out? That Tony Soprano whacked Eunice Goodson?"

"No. But I think I figured out who did. I have to call Betty and Illuminada. We have to go back to the Big Apple Peel. But first, you and I have to talk."

CHAPTER 26

To: Bbarrett@circle.com
From: Mproletariat@ccpw.org
Re: Sol
Date: 11/12/01

Bel, What's with Sol? He gave me some cockamamie excuse about having to baby-sit for his granddaughter the night of the dinner meeting I was telling you about. I hate to bother you, but could you persuade him to change his mind? He's never let us down before. I don't want to worry you, but he doesn't look right. What gives?

Marlene

For someone who "hated" to bother me and didn't want to worry me, Marlene was doing a pretty good job of it. And if she thought Sol didn't look so good the night she had dinner with him, she should have seen his face across the table from me when I told him I thought that Ed had killed both Eunice Goodson and Will Carrington. First Sol blanched, and then he made a low choking sound in his throat. His mouth contorted, and he began to redden. I feared he had swallowed the wrong way and needed the Heimlich maneuver, so I was half out of my seat when he coughed and sputtered and, finally, took a deep breath. I took one myself. I could see him searching for the words to refute my decidedly unwelcome assertion. Apparently he only found one because when, at last, he spoke, all he said was "No."

Few of our neighbors found their way to this Middle Eastern eatery in Weehawken, so there was little chance of any of the hordes of Hoboken homeowners whom Ed had worked for over the years overhearing us. This was just as well because Sol's monosyllabic response had been pretty loud and was accompanied by a glass-rattling bang on the table with his fist. In seconds this was followed by a fairly high-volume accusation. "Bel, you're crazy. You're in over your head with this one, and you don't want to admit it, so you're grasping at straws." Anywhere else people would have thought we were having a fight, but Sol's booming voice was just one in the multilingual chorus of high-decibel conversations that were routine at Beti Kebab.

"I wish I were, Sol. The man has a key to our house," I said quietly. Sol's response had not surprised me. I had expected him to defend Ed and to deny the truth of what I was saying. I didn't blame him. I wished it weren't true myself. But I knew better.

"What possible proof could you have? Why would Ed want to kill anybody?" Sol was toying with his food now, no longer making even a pretense of eating. His questions were reasonable, though, and deserved answers.

"Sol, I don't have any proof yet, but I'm going to get it. I'm going to prove that Ed had motive, method, and opportunity. I think he killed Eunice because he found out she was a stripper and he, like a lot of other religious zealots, thinks stripping is wrong and that strippers are in league with the devil." I helped myself to a mouthful of stuffed eggplant and was relieved to see that Sol had picked up a filo-wrapped cheese stick.

"You're crazy, Bel, you know that," said Sol, pointing his cylinder of filo at me. "You're the one who should be in therapy, not me. You are really way out there on this one, my love. You think the man's a religious zealot just because he listens to a few hymns?" Sol shook his head. "And what motive could Ed possibly have for killing Will Carrington? He didn't even know him."

"Actually he did. They met on the PATH train the night Ed killed Eunice. Andrea said she saw Eunice greet someone when she boarded the train that night. It must have been Ed. Eunice, who was very proper, probably introduced Ed and Will after Will jumped on. Will was the only person who could identify Ed as having been in Eunice's company that night, so when Ed realized Will's name might come up in an investigation, Ed wanted him dead."

Sol broke off a piece of pita bread and dipped it into the tzatziki before he spoke. "Bel, I'm worried about you. You know, I'm not the only one whose worldview has been a little skewed lately." His voice was deep, rich, and gentle, the voice he had courted me with, the voice of the man I had fallen in love with. Except that now what he was saying was dead wrong. "Have you talked to Betty and Illuminada? I'm sure they'll agree that you are really going out on a limb this time."

"I wanted to talk to you first. Then I'll tell them. I knew it was going to be difficult for you to imagine Ed as a murderer, so I wanted to give you a little lead time," I said. "I told them we'd both meet them at Betty's house after dinner."

"Good. I'd like to hear what they have to say. Those two are usually pretty levelheaded," Sol said.

Ignoring the implication embedded in Sol's comment, I signaled the waiter. "May we please have doggy bags for all this?" I asked, pointing at the largely uneaten spread we had ordered. "Maybe our appetites will come back later." While we waited for the check and the leftovers, I sat quietly thinking that maybe levelheadedness was overvalued in our culture. Maybe we needed more people with imagination, people willing to risk being wrong, people who could make connections that defied others, in short, people like me. We had certainly needed them in the CIA and the FBI. Those "levelheaded" investigators had failed to see the dots, let alone connect them. By the time Sol and I arrived at Betty's, I was more convinced than ever that Ed was guilty and that we could prove it.

Once we had all seated ourselves around the coffee table in Betty's comfortable living room and Vic had brought out decaf coffee and tea, Sol said, "So, Bel, unload your latest brainstorm on these people and see what they think."

I looked around at the tired faces of Illuminada, Raoul, Betty, and Vic. I hoped they would feel that the news I bore was worth coming out for on a Monday night. Betty had her Palm Pilot out and was poised to take down whatever I said. I took a deep breath. "Okay. Here's how I see it. Ed Gaines, trusty carpenter for half of Hoboken, is also religious. He listens to hymns all the time. We never thought much about it. Ed meets Eunice when she moves into our neighborhood. He learns that she's a stripper, probably from reading my e-mail and her journal, which I had left around, rather than from the neighbors, because I don't think they knew right away." Sol moved forward in his chair as if he was about to speak, but apparently he thought better of it. I continued. "Ed seems always to know what's on our answering machine too, and Eunice had left messages there as well."

"So what does this have to do with Eunice's murder?" asked Illuminada. She looked pointedly at her watch. "I have to be in court tomorrow at eight." Her impatience made her a particularly tough sell.

"It's complicated, but Ed went to the Big Apple Peel and caught Eunice's show at least once, maybe several times. That's where he got that flyer about the Soprano tours," I said, looking at Sol. "Ed had a flyer of Nelson Vandergast's in his toolbox and we know Nelson left a pile of those at the club, remember?" Betty nodded. Illuminada cocked her head to one side, attentive now. I reached into my purse, took out the flyer I still had there, and handed it to Vic and Raoul, who skimmed it together.

"The night Eunice was killed, her sister Andrea followed her and Will Carrington from the club to the PATH train and saw Eunice greet someone she knew when she got on the train. When Will boarded the train, she and this other person and Will were talking. I'm sure she introduced Will as a hometown friend to this other person. And I'm betting this person was Ed."

"*Como mierda*, Bel. Let me be sure I understand you. This is the guy doing your kitchen in slo-mo? The one who just took off for jury duty? The one you suggested should give me an estimate for work on my mother's porch? Didn't I see him at the block party?" The incredulity in Illuminada's voice as she posed these questions echoed that in Sol's earlier.

I nodded. "Listen," I insisted. "Eunice introduced the two men. Will and Eunice separated either in Hoboken or at one of the other stops, and then Will went back to his hotel or tried to hook up with another woman or who knows what he did. But Ed walked toward her apartment with Eunice who, of course, felt perfectly safe with him." Here I paused, imagining the unsuspecting Eunice, who believed she was walking with a new friend and neighbor. "She never saw it coming when he stabbed her."

I was near tears, and Sol, to his credit, handed me a Kleenex.

"So you figure Ed kills Carrington because he could link him with Eunice?" Illuminada asked. The incredulity was gone from her voice, and she was allowing herself to imagine the scene I had described.

I nodded. Betty said, "But what about jury duty? Ed was on jury duty the night Carrington was killed." Sol smiled at her. He was pleased that she had spotted a snag in

281

the fabric of the scenario I was weaving with my words.

"How do you know he was on jury duty?" asked Raoul. As a CPA, Raoul was familiar with deceptive tactics. He took little for granted.

"We don't," I said. "We only have his word for it. And only his word that he got out early. He's the only person I know who was ever dismissed early from a jury." I tried not to sound smug.

"So you think he made up the jury duty so as to have an excuse to drive to upstate New York and hunt down Carrington and kill him and then drive back here?" asked Sol, running the fingers of each hand through his thinning hair. This question and the familiar nervous gesture reassured me that Sol was beginning to entertain the possibility that Ed was, in fact, guilty. "I suppose we could find out if his pickup was seen up there," he mused, unable to keep his nimble mind from working, even though he loathed the job it was doing. "It's a dark blue Dodge, 1998." He looked at Illuminada as he spoke.

Illuminada nodded and I knew she would attempt to track the car. Betty put down her Palm Pilot and looked up. "We've got several problems," she said. "The biggest is that if this is even a little true, that dude is coming to your house tomorrow to work on your kitchen. If he even thinks you're onto him . . ."

Betty hadn't completed her thought when Vic said, "They're staying here. We're never home. Or you can stay at my place," Vic added, referring to the apartment across town he had maintained since his divorce. "But this is more comfortable and I'm telling you, we're hardly ever here."

"Thanks, both of you," I said. "But Ma and Sofia would never forgive us if we went somewhere else. Besides, Ed won't be suspicious if we just go back to their place."

"So you all really think Bel is onto something about Ed?" Sol asked. "No one in our neighborhood is going to believe it. I'm having trouble myself. I like Ed." He sounded defiant, ready for the disapproval he expected.

"I can find out first thing tomorrow if he served on a jury when he said he did or not," said Illuminada. "And people will have to believe it when we present evidence. As for the fact that you like him, many criminals are likable, but I know, *amigo,* it's not easy to see somebody you thought you knew revealed in another light." Illuminada's voice was gentler than usual, and Sol seemed to take comfort in her words.

"I like Ed too," I said, realizing that in my concern for Sol I had ignored my own feelings of disappointment. "But I also liked Eunice," I added softly. "And I like the Illysarios." Sol looked up. I could tell that he had forgotten

283

about the Illysarios. "Our friend Ed was going to let nineteen-year-old Yronellis Illysario take the rap for him, Sol. So much for his friendship with Charlie. Wait until Tony and Joey P hear that. Not to mention Charlie and Ilona?" Sob was combing his hair again as he realized the depth of Ed's perfidy. "Besides, it's not about liking or not liking," I said, unable to pass up a chance to vent a little of my own anger at the idea of a person who would kill those who threatened his worldview. There were, it seemed, terrorists everywhere.

I squared my shoulders and tried to sound efficient. "I'm going to go back to the club with a picture of Ed to see if anybody there remembers seeing him around. Who knows? He may be stalking some other dancer he's decided doesn't deserve to breathe anymore." The faces of Tiffany and Melanie flashed before me.

"Delphine was taking Polaroids of the kids at the block party after she painted their faces. Later on she got some of us goofing off at the grill. She'll probably post them at the winter block party at Leo's like she did last year. I'll ask her for them," Sol volunteered. "Don't worry. She'll never know why I want them." I squeezed his arm, grateful for his help, grateful for his trust. Maybe he was afraid to return to Manhattan and to fly, but at least he wasn't afraid to face an unwelcome possibility. That was something.

CHAPTER 27

Ed,

Bel and I have gone back to Bel's mother's to stay. Bel needs a little peace and quiet, especially now that it's midterm time and she has exams to read. I'll check in with you after lunch sometime. If you need to reach me before that, Sadie's number is 555-963-1616. We took Virginia Woolf with us, so don't worry about her. Sol

It had been Sol's idea to take Virginia Woolf to Ma's, and I had to admit it was a good one. I'd been so preoccupied with getting together a week's supply of clean clothes and the right books and papers that I'd almost forgotten about her. But I certainly didn't want to leave my beloved pet with a man I suspected of two brutal and premeditated murders. Together and in almost total silence, Sol and I gathered up her things. He took a bag of cat litter and several cans of cat food from the cabinet while I washed her dishes and searched in the debris for her favorite toy. Before long Virginia Woolf's provisions were stacked next to our suitcases by the door.

Ma and Sofia weren't crazy about cat puke

on the carpet and eau de cat litter in the bathroom, but they would understand. Ma had not hesitated when I had called to say we'd like to come back for a few more nights. She had said, "Your room is ready and there's some cold chicken in the fridge." She had said this when I came home from college in the middle of sophomore year nursing a broken heart and terrified I was pregnant. She had said it again years later when I left Lenny even though she thought that was the dumbest thing I had ever done. When I put down the phone, all I could think of was Robert Frost's line "Home is the place where, when you have to go there, they have to take you in." Well, we had to go there.

While I was figuring out what clothes, disks, and books I would need, Sol made a phone call. As soon as I heard him name the person he'd called, I listened carefully to his end of the conversation. "Delphine, Sol Hecht here. We're fine. How're you? Really? In Chelsea? A one-woman show? Sounds like the big time to me. Wouldn't miss it. That'll be one hell of a party. The whole bock'll be there. We'll be on the lookout for the post-card." Sol's voice shifted from a hearty con-gratulatory boom to the more cajoling tone appropriate to requesting a favor. "Listen, Delphine, I'm doing a little art project of my own. It's a surprise. No, you'll see. Don't mention it to anyone, okay? I'll unveil it at the open house Bel and I are going to have when the kitchen is done. Do you still have the Polaroids you took at the block party? The ones you took of the kids and the volley-ball game? And I think you got some of the tables of food and the guys at the grill too?" He hesitated, listening. "Right, I figured the parents would have taken the ones of their kids. But could I borrow the ones you do have for a couple of days? Not to worry, I'll get them back to you. Could I pick them up right now? Bel and I are moving back to her mother's until Ed finishes up." Again he paused, allowing Delphine to pose the inevi-table question. "It's just too chaotic here now for Bel's delicate sensibilities." He listened a moment and then guffawed. "Right. I'll tell her. I'll run over in a couple of minutes. Thanks."

By the time I lured a perplexed and suspi-cious Virginia Woolf into her traveling cage and heaved our stuff into the car, Sol had returned from Delphine's with the photos. We decided to wait until we were at Ma's to look at them. When we pulled out of our vest-pocket parking lot, Virginia Woolf was meowing miserably in her cage. Although we were only going a few blocks and to a fa-miliar destination, I felt like a refugee fleeing for my very life.

Things seemed less dramatic when we ar-

287

rived back at the grandkid room at Ma and Sofia's that we had occupied only a few days before. Ma and Sofia, hosts at our own private elder hostel, were asleep. We unpacked and put away our things in the two lined bureau drawers that weren't already filled with heating pads, donut pillows, an outmoded toilet-seat extender, and other devices used to either warm, cushion, or support the frail bodies of the elderly. I slammed shut a bureau drawer full of Depends, but not before it struck me, and not for the first time, that in recent years the grand-kid room had devolved into a storage facility for Ma and Sofia's growing collection of surgical supply products. I flashed on the fact that my mother was aging rapidly, my beloved was cracking up, and across the Hudson there was enough thick white dust to make the fallout at our house look like a sprinkling of confectioner's sugar. While I showered, I tamped these depressing thoughts down into the depths of denial where they belonged.

While Sol showered, I made hot chocolate and took the Tupperware container of roasted chicken out of the fridge. Since we had forgotten our doggy bag on the table at Beti Kebab, we made short work of the chicken and cocoa. Thus fortified, Sol and I went through Delphine's Polaroids. I was startled when I saw a photo of a smiling Eunice standing behind the vegetarian table with Tanya and Ignacia. At the sight of the doomed young woman I felt myself choking up. Just then Sol exclaimed, "Here's one of Ed!" At once I banished my sadness, condemning it to consort with my visions of Ma in a wheelchair and Sol in a straitjacket in the nether regions of my consciousness. Across the kitchen table Sol was holding up a snapshot of Joey P, himself, and Ed, all three brandishing barbecue tongs and mugging for the camera.

"That'll do if it's the only one. But let's see if we can find one of him where he's not making a face," I said. We continued to go through the pictures and found not one but three that we both agreed would be useful. In the first Ed was carrying a tray of hot dogs to a table. In the second he was breaking up ice in the trash can containing soft drinks prior to refilling it from the cartons stacked next to him. I shuddered, newly aware of his malevolent strength. And then it hit me. I shuddered again, now because I knew I was looking at the weapon that had pierced Eunice's heart. I hardly glanced at the last photo in which Ed stood with Charlie, apparently watching the volleyball game from the sidelines.

"Sol," I squealed, trying to keep my voice down. "He killed her with the ice pick. I know it. She was pierced through the heart. Ohmigod."

Sol looked thoughtful and reexamined the photo I was pointing to. "We use the same ice pick every year. I think it was Charlie's father's. You don't see those much anymore." Then he looked up at me and said, "We store all the barbeque utensils in Felice's shed. Joey P usually scrubs them and boxes them, and Felice keeps them there with the other stuff. Want me to take a look tomorrow? See if it's there? Can't hurt."

"It would be a big help," I said, glad he thought of it and even gladder I wouldn't have to make time to rummage through Felice's shed looking for a murder weapon that I was almost certain wouldn't be there. It would be good to be totally certain. "A really big help."

Then it was my turn to work the phone. I called Tiffany and Melanie. Their schedules were so erratic that I didn't concern myself about waking them. Tiffany's machine picked up, and I left a message, but Melanie's voice greeted me after only two rings. "Hi, Melanie. Bel Barrett here. I'm so glad I caught you. Can you and Tiffany meet me tomorrow afternoon around five? Just for a minute or two? No, not at the club. At the sushi place we went to last time, the one near the Waxworks, okay? It's important."

"Yeah, sure. I don't start dancing tomorrow until six and I think Tiff finishes about five. That'll work for us," she said. "You take care now," she added before hanging up. Her admonition echoed in my ears all night. Even the familiar clay dinosaurs and Lucite-framed pictures of Sofia's snaggle-toothed great grandchildren did little to reassure me. I slept fitfully at best and left early for school, leaving Sol to consume the omelet Sofia was whipping up for us.

In spite of little sleep and less breakfast, the day had begun well. Illuminada had called and said, "*Chiquita,* you were right about the jury duty. He wasn't there." Having my hunch confirmed reenergized me. I read and graded a whole set of midterms while giving another class their exams. It was only when I went to record the exam grades I had just assigned that I realized my grade book was not in my book bag.

Losing one's grade book at midterm exam time is to a professor what losing one's passport during wartime is to a foreign correspondent — a disaster, perhaps an irrevocable one. Heedless of the students milling around me to hand in their blue books, I muttered, "Damn," and began to empty the contents of my book bag onto the desk. Although my imprecation didn't do a bit of good, I repeated it until the bag lay there deflated next to a heap of assorted books and folders bulging with papers. There was no sign of my missing grade book. I flipped through the folders to make sure it hadn't slipped into one of them. It hadn't. Many of my colleagues entered their grades and attendance records on their computers, but alas, I had not made this leap. I still preferred the time-honored ritual of recording students' grades and absences by hand in little boxes to typing this data into my PC where, I feared, it would disappear whenever that moody machine decided to crash. "Well, that'll teach you, you hopeless Luddite," I muttered to myself. "Next semester, Bel Barrett, you put everything on your PC, and you back it up on floppies and CDs every day. End of discussion." After gathering up my things, I exited the room, still castigating myself under my breath.

Back in my office, I scoured the tiny cubicle searching for the missing record book. When I was down on my hands and knees looking beneath my office mate's desk, I realized that I'd probably left the damn book back at the house the night before when we had made our escape. I could visualize it on the table next to my computer. I remember being about to toss it into my book bag when Sol had asked me where Virginia Woolf's toy was, and I'd begun to search on the floor for that. In the flurry of finding the toy and trying to assemble a few presentable and appropriate outfits for the week ahead, I'd forgotten all about my grade book. This realization came with the shock of the body blow I'd experienced the time I'd driven off leaving the infant Rebecca in the shopping cart in the supermarket parking lot. "Double damn," I muttered and picked up the phone to call Sol. He could get the grade book when he stopped by the house today to talk to Ed. "Damn, damn, damn," I swore when I realized that Sol's cell phone wasn't turned on. Desperate, I called our house to leave a message there for Sol. I was sure Sol would check messages on our home phone from his cell phone before too long.

The hairs on my neck and arms stood on end when Ed himself answered the phone, his customary cheery and helpful persona a sharp contrast with the Jack the Ripper he'd become in my mind. "Oh. It's you, Professor. I'm expectin' the guy who's going to wire the dishwasher to get back to me. That's why I picked up. What can I do for you?"

"Ed," I answered, struggling to sound as if I were talking to a trusted carpenter rather than a serial killer. "Has Sol stopped by yet? I'd like to ask him to pick up my grade book. I think I left it next to my PC."

"Sorry, Professor. He was here, and he checked out the new dishwasher. It came this morning. He picked up some mail and your newspapers. He left about half an hour ago," Ed said, sounding really apologetic. "Wanna hold on and I'll have a look-see? If it's there, I can drop it off at your mother's later." The whole conversation was surreal. Here I was talking about dishwashers and mail with a man I'd known for years, whom, as it turned out, I hadn't really known at all. A killer offering to run errands!

"No, thanks, Ed. Don't bother. I'll pick it up on my way home tonight," I said, so preoccupied with keeping this ghoul away from Sadie and Sofia that I let him know I'd be at our own house later on. Not a gifted move because if he even suspected that I suspected him . . . but he didn't.

It was just five that afternoon when I entered the Japanese restaurant on Fourteenth Street in Manhattan. I sat down and ordered a bowl of soba noodles and a few shrimp tempura in seafood stock. I was in no mood to gnaw on seaweed, raw fish, or cold rice that night. I wanted comfort food, and the thick soba noodles in the hot broth would not disappoint. Tiffany and Melanie walked in just as my hotpot came. They placed orders for tea and sushi before they even sat down. Tiffany was pale under her tan, and her gray sweats only accentuated her pallor. Her eyes were ringed and her sandy hair lank. "You look tired," I said by way of greeting.

"Late night. Lost a patient yesterday. Nice woman. Lots of paperwork," said Tiffany, yawning and covering her mouth with fingers tipped with silver nails. "Didn't feel much like dancing today, let me tell you."

"Sorry," I said, wondering what it must be like to be Florence Nightingale and a floozie in the same twenty-four-hour period. "Hi, Melanie," I said, noting that Melanie, whose shift at the Big Apple Peel was about to begin, looked pretty bouncy compared to Tiffany, who had just finished hers. I guess all that gyrating and writhing took a toll too.

"Hey, Professor. What's up?" Melanie asked, checking her watch. "Sorry to be rushing you, but I'm onstage in exactly fifty-five minutes and I've got to do the glue and glitter bit first." She glanced down at her substantial chest bulging beneath her Polartec jacket and sighed at the effort involved in showing it off.

"I'd like you to look at some pictures and tell me if you've ever seen this guy around the club. If you two don't recognize him, I want you to run the pictures by Daphne and see if she does," I said, fumbling in my purse for the envelope of photos. I had a moment of panic that, like my grade book, they might not be where they were supposed to be, but it dissipated as soon as my fingers found the envelope.

"Why don't you take the photos to Daphne yourself like you did last time?" Tiffany asked.

"Yeah. That way you can ask her questions like you did then," said Melanie.

"Because this guy knows me. If he's frequenting the club at all and sees me there . . ." I broke off mid-sentence.

"Got it," said Tiffany. She picked up the envelope of photos I placed on the table and opened it. She and Melanie literally put their heads together and stared at the Polaroids. At the sight of the first one, the one of Ed carrying a tray of hot dogs, they looked at each other and nodded. Tiffany flipped quickly through the others, holding them so both women could view them. It was clear to me even before they spoke that they had recognized Ed right away. "He's been in a few times recently, but I don't remember seeing him before Eunice died," said Tiffany, pointing to Ed's mugging face in the photo with Joey P and Sol.

"Me either. And that's odd, because he's becoming sort of a regular of mine these days," said Melanie slowly, paling now beneath her tan as the sinister implications of Ed's interest began to dawn on her. With her black hair tied back in a ponytail and her even features innocent of makeup, she looked like a schoolgirl.

That's why I was not surprised when Tiffany said, "Mel's taken over Eunice's routine in the Academy for a couple of shifts a week. Meet the new Professor." Melanie, executed a mock bow from across the table. "So she inherited a lot of Eunice's regulars, the

296

teacher's pets, but this guy . . ."

"He's new," Melanie interjected. Both women had dug into their sushi when it arrived, but Melanie stopped eating as soon as she eyeballed the photos. She put her chopsticks down and said, "Want to finish mine, Tiff? I'm kinda full. I can't dance on a full stomach." She pushed her plate toward Tiffany.

"You don't want to get a doggy bag?" asked Tiffany, eyeing the small slabs of tuna and salmon atop their pillows of rice.

"No, go ahead, take it," said Melanie.

Tiffany did, her appetite apparently unaffected by the prospect of a killer frequenting her workplace, perhaps in the process of selecting his next victim. "I need energy to think about this," she explained. "And I've just been dancing for four hours straight." In between bites, Tiffany looked at me over the rim of her teacup and asked, "So now what? The cops?"

Melanie greeted her friend's words with only, "Duh," as if bringing in the police at this point were the only logical thing to do.

In the spirit of the monosyllabic dialogue she had introduced, I replied, "Not." Only when both their heads flew up did I elaborate. "Not quite yet, that is. This guy is very well thought of in New Jersey where he lives. He's a highly respected carpenter who has worked for a lot of important people. He's a

297

churchgoer and active in his community. People like him." Tiffany's shoulders slumped as I continued, and Melanie's eyes widened with a combination of fear and incredulity. "And," I continued, "the police are still totally involved with the aftermath of the terrorism."

"So what am I supposed to do?" said Melanie. "Just keep dancing until some night he follows me out of here and slits my throat while I'm walking to the train?"

"Not exactly," I said, leaning across the table. "I've got a better plan."

CHAPTER 28

To: Professor Bel Barrett
From: President Woodman
Re: Special assignment
Date: 11/13/01 08:12:44

Bel,

Would like an update ASAP on how you are progressing on your special assignment. Need to report to the Trustees at next Tues. mtg. Hope to see you in my office by the end of this week. Don't let me down on this one.

Ron

On the train on the way home from New York I read the mail I'd grabbed from my mailbox and stuffed in my bag. Woodman's memo was hardly surprising. The board was still making his life difficult because we'd had a stripper on the RECC faculty. That she had been an excellent instructor didn't matter to the Gang of Twelve. That she'd danced naked, been murdered, and made headlines did. So Woodman was passing the pressure on to me. Well, I would have some good news for him soon because what I'd told Tiffany and Melanie was true. I did have a plan.

But implementing it would have to wait. First I had to get my grade book. I had debated asking Sol to pick it up the next day, but I knew I wouldn't rest easy until I had the damn thing back in my possession. What if it wasn't where I thought it was and I had to really search for it? He wouldn't know where to look. It made sense to go back and find it myself and then walk the few blocks to Ma and Sofia's. The darkened house was quiet when I put the key in the familiar lock. Once in, I flipped on the lights. Something was different. There was yet another huge box in the kitchen, probably the new dishwasher. Carefully I picked my way through the cartons, stacks of windows, and half-built cabinets until I reached the steps.

Once upstairs in our bedroom, I went straight to my computer and gingerly lifted the dropcloth that covered it. Wrinkling my nose at the all-too-familiar chalky smell of plaster particles, I gently and slowly lowered the sheet of plastic to the floor, trying not to expose my poor PC to the deadly dust film that clouded the cloth. I saw my grade book at once, right where I had thought it would be. Relief made me smile. *Silly to be so retro,* I thought, resolving again to computerize my record-keeping next semester. With one hand

I clutched my grade book to my chest while with the other I reached down to pick up the dropcloth.

"Don't bother, Professor. I'll get that," said Ed, looming in the doorway. He wore chinos and a white button-down shirt and held one of his smaller toolboxes in one hand. I pictured the wooden-handled ice pick inside it next to the hammers, wrenches, and screwdrivers, like a viper in a cage of gerbils at the mall pet shop. Seeing my face blanch, he added. "Sorry, Professor. Didn't mean to scare you."

Remember, he doesn't know you know, I told myself. *Try to sound normal.* "Well, you did." There seemed no harm in stating the obvious. *Why hadn't he hollered to let me know he was in the house? He probably thought that would frighten me more,* I rationalized. "What on earth are you doing here at this hour, working overtime?"

"Nah. I probably should though to make up for the days I had jury duty, right?" Ed's grin faded as he explained. "I came over to get a few of my tools." He held up the box. I tried not to think about the ice pick, to listen as he explained his after-hours presence in my house, in my bedroom. "Somebody musta tried to break inta my apartment, pried apart a couple a the bars on my basement window. I wanta see if I can straighten 'em out myself or if I gotta call an iron worker." As he

301

spoke, Ed entered the cluttered bedroom and stood on the other side of the computer station between me and the door. He reached down and grabbed one end of the plastic sheet.

"Easy, Ed," I said, not relinquishing my hold on the other end. "This thing's full of dust. I don't want to shake it. That's it. Thank you," I said as together we shrouded the PC once again. I hoped he had not noticed the trembling of my hand or the quaver in my voice.

"Glad you found your book, Professor," he said, not moving.

"Me too. Sorry you had an attempted break-in. That's really scary. I sure hope whoever did it isn't going to make the rounds of the neighborhood." I faked a series of sneezes and, sucking in my gut, edged around him quickly. "Boy, this dust is really getting to me. I'm outta here. Good luck with fixing your bars. And you think about that overtime," I called over my shoulder, trying to sound breezily casual while racing down the stairs and out the door. I kept racing until I got to Ma's.

Illuminada and Betty were already there along with Raoul and Vic. Sol was in the kitchen with Sofia and Ma making decaf and heating water for tea. When he finally joined us around the dining room table, Sofia and Ma stayed in the kitchen sharing the local paper and shaking their heads over the latest bad news. I knew they'd go upstairs soon to watch more bad news on television. I didn't begrudge them the chance to eavesdrop on our strategy session for a few minutes. Ma's career as a court stenographer in Brooklyn had left her with an appetite for intrigue.

"When I stopped by our house tonight to look for my gradebook, Ed showed up," I said. There was a highly gratifying collective gasp. I continued. "He claimed to be picking up a few tools to repair some damage done to his window bars by a would-be burglar. But I think Ed is moving in on another dancer, probably a young woman named Melanie, who has replaced Eunice in the specialty room where she danced. He needed his toolbox because he keeps the murder weapon in there." More gasps greeted this assertion.

"What kind of tool does he use, a long nail?" asked Illuminada. "That would work because the police report says Will Carrington died of a puncture wound in the chest, same as Eunice."

"Bel noticed that in one of the photos we have of Ed from the block party, he was breaking up the hunks of congealed ice in a trash can where we keep soft drinks. For years PANA has used an old wooden-handled ice pick of Charlie Illysario's to do that. We store it with the barbeque tools in Felice Aquino's shed. I looked for it this morning.

303

It's not there," Sol said. I could tell from his serious tone that he was pleased to have a contribution to make to the conversation as well as to the investigation.

"So Ed's on his way to New York now to kill another stripper? OhmiGod. Shouldn't we be doing something?" Betty had her cell phone out, ready to call in the NYPD.

"Not to worry," I assured her, although I had had the same reaction when I realized that we wouldn't be able to mobilize that night. "I told Melanie to call in sick tonight, just to be on the safe side. She called Queenie, the housemother, the one who does the scheduling. Melanie called in right from the restaurant where we were and said she had a stomach flu. Then she went straight home. So if Ed goes to the Big Apple Peel later tonight, he won't find her there." I leaned back in my chair and sipped my tea, pleased with my own foresight.

"Do you really think he'll go tonight?" asked Raoul. "Don't you believe his story about the burglar?"

"Yes and no. Yes, I do think he's going there tonight. And no, I don't believe his burglary story. He picked up his toolbox, but he wasn't dressed to wrestle with window bars," I said. "Besides, I passed his apartment on my way up the street. The bars are twisted, but they've been like that for months. If we could get ourselves together to go to the Big Apple Peel tonight, I'm sure we would find him there."

"I'm ready," said Vic. "I've always wanted to go to one of those places." A grin flashed across his face and disappeared when Betty swatted him playfully on the arm.

"The holdup is with Illuminada's end of things," I said. At the mention of her name, Illuminada looked up from her coffee cup. "She needs at least a few hours lead time to arrange our backup," I explained. "I promised Melanie a lot of backup. In fact, I promised Melanie a ringer." When I heard Illuminada sigh, I knew that she understood what I meant. She would have to call in favors from cops she knew on both sides of the Hudson to come up with one to cooperate with us this time. Fortunately over the years she had done a lot of favors for the girls and boys in blue. "Okay, *chiquita,* tell me, what does she look like? I'll see whose arms I can twist."

By the time I had finished outlining what was really a very simple plan, one thing was clear. This time, Sol wasn't going to be in on it. Vic had said, "So Sol, what clothes should I bring for you? You want to be a cool CEO type in an Armani suit? I got a charcoal one that's about your size. The widow brought down two suits. The Armani made her husband look kind of gray, so we put him in the other one. She never came back for the Armani. Or you want to be a woman? I've

305

got a lime green silk sheath that is really you." Sol smiled faintly at his friend's macabre humor.

"I don't think so, Vic. Not my color. Seriously, I'm sitting this one out right here Thanks, though." Sol's smile flickered and died. Without it his face looked like that of an old man, lined and sad-eyed. Seeing him so diminished hurt my heart, and I reached over and stroked his arm.

"No problem," said Vic, glancing quickly at Betty. Then the two couples telegraphed each other knowing looks. I was sure they had all discussed Sol's post-traumatic stress disorder, and I appreciated their tact. I still felt sad though, and the feeling persisted after everyone left when Sol and I brought the coffee cups into the kitchen. To my surprise, Ma and Sofia were still up. If they noticed my blue mood, they said nothing. While I loaded the dishwasher, I reminded myself that if Sol had passed up the chance to help out Marlene because doing so meant going to Manhattan, it had been silly of me to expect him to brave the city to trap a killer. Sol had his own demons to confront, and he wasn't ready.

CHAPTER 29

To: Bbarrett@circle.com
From: Nvandergast@earthlink.net
Re: absence and project
Date: 11/14/01 18:59:48

Professor Barrett,

Sorry, but I'm taking a personal day tomorrow, so I'm going to miss the Faculty
Development Seminar as well as a couple
of my own classes. A group of hotshot
diplomats from the UN is scheduled to
take a Soprano Safari luncheon tour and a
TV newscaster's going to shoot a few minutes of it for the six o'clock news. This
could be my big break. The outline for my
project is attached. Thanks for your understanding. See you on the news!

Nelson

Nelson's e-mail message was the first one I
saw the next morning at work. Why had he
scheduled an important tour on a day when
he had to teach? This would be something to
discuss with him when we went over the
skimpy outline for his ambitious project ten-

tatively entitled "Motivating the Marketing Student: How to Spin Spinning." Fortunately my classes went smoothly. In one speech class I gave back exams and conferred with students about their progress and plans for improvement. In the other I listened to students give their second talk of the semester and took notes so I could offer useful feedback. And in the Faculty Development Seminar I led a discussion on testing. There had been no time all day to worry about how things would go that evening.

According to Sol, Ma and Sofia had been out all afternoon. I had harbored the faint hope that at the last minute Sol would change his mind and go into New York with us, but he hadn't. When Illuminada and Raoul picked me up that night, Sol sat hunkered over the radio listening to NPR. He kissed me goodbye and turned up the volume. We drove straight to the funeral home to meet Vic and Betty.

Once in Vic's office, we tore into the still-warm pizzas Betty had provided "so nobody would have to drink on an empty stomach."

Illuminada said, "Well, *amigos,* I've got a ringer." She shook her head. "It wasn't easy, let me tell you. *Dios mío,* everybody's working overtime these days. I had to call in a favor from 1994," she said, laughing. "That's the year I dug up the evidence that enabled a rookie cop, Mariluisa Reyes, to make her first real drug collar stick. Her mother and Mamacita go way back to Havana, so I did it for free. Some two-bit dealer Mariluisa brought in was out on bail. I actually followed that *hombre* myself and took pictures of him selling crack in a lot next to a middle school on First Avenue." Illuminada raised her hands to her eyes, extending her thumbs and index fingers in the shape of a camera. With her index finger she repeatedly pressed an imaginary button. "Yes!" She raised her small fist at the memory of this long-ago triumph. "So Mariluisa's a captain now in a precinct in the West Village. I gave her the whole story, and as we speak, she's over at the Big Apple Peel briefing everybody on what's going to happen and telling them what to do. She won't even have to wear a wig since she's got long black hair. I think she's about the right height too." Illuminada wiped her fingers on a napkin and helped herself to one of the bottles of water Vic offered.

Because Ed might have remembered him from the block party, Raoul wore a blond wig. It changed him from an incredibly handsome dark-haired man to an incredibly handsome light-haired one. Vic didn't need a disguise because, as he put it, undertakers were just as lecherous as the rest of the male population, so even if Ed had been to a funeral or two at Vallone and Sons and did recognize him, it didn't matter. Illuminada and Betty wore the same disguises they had worn the first evening we went to the Big Apple Peel. But, to Illuminada's great relief, this time Betty carried a cane instead of using a wheelchair. I too reverted to my former persona, that of a horny Russian pit musician out on the town. In an effort to get into the role, I named myself Boris.

Daphne, who had been briefed by Mariluisa, admitted us as we drifted in. She took our money, and smiled her seductive smile. She did not seem put off when Vic gaped at her cleavage. She handed each of us a Soprano Safari brochure with our change. In other words, she treated us exactly the same way she treated every other customer. Under my wig I was sweating but my palms were icy. It was unlikely that Ed would recognize people he'd met only once, but he knew me well, had been in my home every day for months. What if he wasn't fooled by my wig or my beard or my phony Russian phrases? Suppose he realized that Boris was Bel and that Bel was on to him? What then? I took a few deep breaths, ordered Boris a Smirnoff on the rocks, and stared at the dancers.

Tiffany, who was near the center of the line, paused in front of Vic and removed her tassels just as Illuminada and Betty took seats at a table across from mine. Vic's jaw hung open as Tiffany's large tan breasts and

310

blue sequined nipples swayed inches from his now protruding eyeballs. I glanced at Betty who had her hand over her mouth. Was she laughing or struggling to keep from telling him to shut his mouth and put his eyes back in his head? By the time Vic had collected himself enough to insert a bill under the elastic of Tiffany's white spangled thong, Betty and Illuminada had disappeared behind the door of the Academy. Still holding my vodka, I followed them into the room.

To the amplified tune of "School Days, School Days," Melanie strode around the small stage brandishing a long pointer in one hand and an outsized grade book in the other. She wore a mortarboard and an academic gown. Her black hair had been wound into an austere bun at the nape of her neck, and her rounded eyes peered at us from behind glasses with large, square, tortoise-shell frames. Every now and then she would stop and pretend to inscribe something in her grade book with a quill pen held in place by a glittering red garter half way up her thigh. Sometimes she would point at a given spectator, wag her index finger at him, extricate her pen, and write something in her book. At an appropriate time in the song she swirled over to the blackboard and erased the writing on it. Every motion of her arms caused her robe to part, affording us a glimpse of cleavage or a flash of thigh. Then she wrote something on the board. When she swirled to face us again, she swirled right out of her gown. But I was not really paying much attention to Melanie's antics.

That was because before I realized it I had seated myself at a desk next to one occupied by Nelson Vandergast. What was he doing here tonight? He hadn't been able to teach or to attend the Faculty Development Seminar this afternoon, so what was he doing here now? Before my inner professor got too involved in judging Nelson's priorities, I reminded myself of why I was there and felt sweat beading on my forehead and drenching my whole upper body. Boris was having a hot flash. And it wasn't just an ordinary hot flash either. It was one of those retro ones that post-menopausal women wearing low-dose estrogen patches only get when they are under extraordinary stress. And I was stressed out for sure now. What if Nelson recognized me? I threw back a slug of vodka, choking as it burned its way down my throat, and shrank into my chair. Just then Nelson reached out and slipped a bill through the slot in the window separating the students in the Academy from their teacher.

Melanie's black hair had escaped from the bun and spun around as she reached beneath it and slowly took off her glasses. Before I could focus on her next move, three more men entered the room. I sensed their presence before I saw them. When I turned to check them out, I saw Vic first. He took one look at the nearly naked Melanie and sank into the nearest empty desk. Next I saw Ed. He walked past me to a vacant front seat in the row next to mine. I could see the stern line of his mouth and the way one of his ears twitched whenever Melanie bent over. There was no sign of his easy affability, his ready smile. He carried a dark green canvas shoulder bag. Was that where he had stashed the ice pick? I shivered through my sweat. The third man to join us was Raoul. Unlike Vic, he looked slightly bored or, perhaps, a little drunk. I knew he was neither.

Ed reached into his shoulder bag. I froze, my glass halfway to my mouth. Melanie missed a beat as she removed first one of Eunice's high white boots and then the other. But Ed had wanted only to get a bill with which to feed the slot. He inserted the bill without taking his narrowed eyes off Melanie. I thought it was time for Boris to part with a five, so I took a rumpled one from my pocket and made my way to the window, sweating through my too-tight sports bra as I walked. When I resumed my seat, I felt better. Neither Nelson nor Ed had paid any attention to the slightly tipsy Boris. What seemed like hours went by until Melanie, again fully clad in her academic regalia, curtseyed and left the small stage. School was out.

There was a mass exodus from the Academy. I let Nelson pass ahead of me, not wanting to press my luck by stepping in front of him. An olive-skinned man in a Nehru jacket and a black man in a golden robe and plumed headdress followed him. I hadn't noticed them before. Had Nelson brought the UN types to the club or were these just standard-issue tourists? I remained seated until Ed stood and lumbered out, his green shoulder bag dark against his white shirt. As soon as he left the room, I left too. I followed him into the men's room, barely noticing the looks Vic and Raoul shot me. Realizing that Boris was ill equipped to function appropriately at the urinal, I stepped into a stall and stayed a decent interval. When I flushed and emerged, Ed had left and Nelson stood at the urinal, his back to me, his head down. It was awhile before I saw him again. Not wanting to miss the final act of the drama we had so carefully staged, I left the Big Apple Peel and stood beneath the awning at the door.

In a few minutes a crowd of dancers burst out of the club, swinging bags of gear and chattering in the manner of young people leaving the workplace after a long hard shift. In the center of the group, talking and laughing, was the now very familiar dark-haired figure. Instead of an academic robe, she wore a black leather jacket and black jeans. Her hair was in the ponytail she apparently favored when not on stage. She wore brown clogs. Over one shoulder, she had slung an enormous red, white, and blue nylon sack, which she held onto with both hands. She looked like a hip and patriotic Santa Claus.

The dancers ignored the cabs queued up outside the club waiting for fares. I ignored them too and crossed the street, moving into the shadows cast by the doorways of buildings. Several other figures glided silently in and out of these shadows too. I recognized Raoul, Vic, and Nelson Vandergast. For the second time that evening, I asked myself what the hell he was doing there. Then he was gone, leaving only Raoul and Vic moving stealthily forward. On the other side of Fourteenth Street the dancers headed west, and at the corner all but one descended the stairs to the subway. They waved good-bye to the woman with the ponytail, who still walked west but now walked alone.

Thanks to the streetlights, I could watch her striding down the empty street, her red, white, and blue bag bobbing up and down with each step. I watched as a large man holding something in his hand, approached from behind, overtook her, and pivoted to face her. For a second they stood frozen like figures dancing on a music box. Then he raised his hand over his head. My heart

315

stopped. I wanted to scream a warning. When a woman's voice rang out, at first I thought it was mine. "Stop or I'll shoot. Hold it right there. You're under arrest." Illuminada jumped out of a cab parked curbside that she had entered from the street while the crowd separated at the subway. Betty had arranged to have that cab there and it had served its purpose well. Illuminada stood arm's length from Ed with her feet apart, holding her gun with both hands and aiming it straight at his chest.

"Drop that weapon," ordered Mariluisa. In the time it took the ice pick to clatter to the pavement, she had whipped a badge out of her jacket pocket and stuck it in his face, now the face of a man having a bad dream from which he is unable to awaken. In another second she had removed handcuffs from her bag and was snapping them around his wrists, all the while reading him his rights in the singsong monotone of the veteran police officer in a grade-B movie. In the distance, I saw Vic and Betty making their way along Fourteenth Street paying off the cabbies Betty had stationed on each block because we hadn't been sure at what point Ed would make his move. Behind me I saw Nelson Vandergast trotting toward the PATH station.

CHAPTER 30

"Harlots do the work of the devil."
"I do God's work on earth."
"Vengeance is mine, sayeth the Lord."
"Daughter of Eve, you are damned."

"According to Mariluisa, Queenie collected the money clients put in the slots each night, and one night last week she noticed that some of the bills from the Academy had these weird messages scrawled in the margins. She and Mike turned them in, but the cops didn't have a detective they could spare to hang out at the club and look into it. Pretty creepy, no?" Everybody assumed my question was rhetorical, so nobody bothered to answer it. The five of us were sprawled in Ma and Sofia's living room, reliving the highlights of the evening's work.

"Why the long face, girlfriend? I'd think you'd be happy that you were proved right. We know how you love to be right. President Woodman will be thrilled. Your neighbors whose daughter was accused will be relieved and happy . . ." Betty's words trailed off as she waited for me to explain why I alone of the group was not wallowing in self-satisfaction and self-congratulation.

"Yes, *chiquita*, and the cops on this side of the river will be once again in your debt. I know how you love to outsmart the cops," said Illuminada, whose delight in solving cases that stymied the police rivaled my own. "*Dios mío*, let me see at least a little smile. Think how much safer all those dancers are now with that sick hombre locked up. Even what's her name, Eunice's sister, is going to thank you for helping to put him away."

I'd forgotten all about Andrea. I'd have to call the Gotham Center and arrange to see her, so I could tell her in person. I could deliver her damn boxes while I was at it. But even the thought of bringing this news to Andrea did not force my compressed lips into a smile or stop my eyes from darting toward the door. "Well, in case you haven't noticed, nobody's here. I can't imagine where they'd all be at this hour. Sol's just not himself lately. There's no note and no message on the machine . . ." Now my own voice faded as I debated how long to wait before calling the emergency room at St. Mary's.

"Maybe Sol took the Odd Couple to a movie," Vic offered, trying to be helpful.

"Or to Newport Mall to do some early holiday shopping," suggested Raoul. "Mamacita started her Christmas shopping already."

"Maybe he took them to the Senior Center for an event," said Illuminada.

318

"At this hour?" I snapped. It was well after midnight. I reached for the phone. "I'm going to call . . ." There was a scraping sound, the noise of a key in the old lock. Suddenly the door swung open to reveal Charlie Illysario, who waved Sofia in. Sofia held two canes, her own and Ma's. Behind her strode Sol carrying Ma, her small bird-boned body barely straining his arms. *OhmiGod, she's had a stroke,* I thought. *She's passed out somewhere. Maybe she's had a heart attack. Why didn't he take her to the ER?* Then I saw her eyes. They caught mine and she closed one slowly in an unmistakable wink.

Raoul and Illuminada jumped off the sofa so Sol could lower Ma to it, while Charlie arranged the dice-shaped throw pillows beneath her legs. It was only then that I noticed the bandage wound around her ankle. "OhmiGod, Ma. You've broken your ankle," I said, only too aware of her diminished bone density. "Did you go to St. Mary's? Who set it?"

"Relax, love. It's just a bad sprain," said Sol.

"A sprain? How did . . ." I began.

"Your hotshot mother and her sidekick here," Charlie pointed at Sofia as he spoke. "They couldn't wait for . . ."

"Now, Charlie, don't you make Bel feel guilty," said Ma. These were the first words she had uttered since her dramatic entrance.

"That's my job." I was relieved to see that Ma's sense of humor had survived whatever it was that had happened to her, but disturbed that somehow Ma's injury was my fault.

"An hour or so after you left, the phone rang, and . . ." Sol began.

"And this is my story, too, so let me tell it," said Ma. Betty had vacated her chair for Sofia, whose face wore the same tired but triumphant expression it had after, in defiance of her doctor's advice, she made four trays of eggplant parm, labeled them neatly, and stacked them on a freezer shelf. Sol sat at the end of the sofa next to Ma's feet, and the rest of us pulled in chairs from the dining room. Even Illuminada, whose appetite for narrative decreased as the hour latened, leaned toward Ma, prepared to listen. "Sofia and I got tired of waiting for Bel or Sofia's daughter to make the time to take us to Ground Zero, so we went by ourselves." She cast a defiant glance around the room as if daring any of us to say she was too old to go into the city by herself anymore. No one said a word. "We took a cab to the PATH train here and got off in the Village."

When Ma paused for breath, Sofia chimed in. "We bought some flowers at a shop on Christopher Street to bring with us."

Ma tolerated this interruption and continued. "Yes, golden mums. So then we took another cab downtown." She paused again, no doubt remembering how easy it used to be to take the PATH or the ferry to the World Trade Center from Hoboken. "And we got the driver to let us off as close as he could, which was on Fulton and Broadway. It was very strange to be there, you know, without those buildings." She took a deep breath. "So we crossed Broadway, and we got as close as we could to where they are clearing away the debris. We couldn't get too close though because it was quite crowded. We walked along the fence with the other tourists and looked at the memorials. Sofia put our bouquet down with all the others." Now Ma paused to brush away a tear.

"We were getting ready to cross the street again and try to get a cab back uptown when I tripped on the curb," said Ma.

"Yes," said Sofia. "She tripped and went down. Thank God there was a nice lady there . . ."

"Sofia," Ma scolded, not wanting to share the floor at what was clearly the story's high point.

"I felt this sharp pain in my ankle, and I couldn't get up. But this nice lady, a tourist from Nebraska, had a cell phone and she called 911. An ambulance came and took me to St. Vincent's. We had to wait hours before they took care of me because there were so many other more seriously ill people there. There had been a bad car accident earlier in the afternoon. It got late, and I knew Sol would be worried, so Sofia called him just to tell him that I hurt my ankle and where we were. Next thing I know, he and Charlie are there in the waiting room with us for no reason at all." Ma rolled her eyes to indicate how unnecessary it had been for Sol and Charlie to come to the hospital. "Sofia told him we were going to take a cab home. But no. Sol has to schlep all the way in to New York like I'm an invalid or something." She was doing her best to sound indignant, but I could tell from the way her eyes had filled again that she was really pleased. "And he brings Charlie. The two of them brought us pizza and sat with us until the doctor examined me and X-rayed my ankle, and then they drove us home. This one," here she jerked her head at Sol, "wouldn't even let me walk to the car or to the house. End of story."

"I got Charlie to come along because I didn't know if they'd lifted the restrictions on driving through the tunnel without passengers yet. I didn't want to get hassled and have to come back for him." Sol spoke casually as if his return to Manhattan were not a big deal, as if driving through the Lincoln Tunnel were something he had not had qualms about. "I was going to take a cab in, but

Charlie charges a lot less," Sol added. I knew he had welcomed his friend's company on this trip that was at once a rescue mission and an exercise in facing his demons.

"So that's enough about me," said Ma. "Now tell us what happened tonight." By the time we recounted how we had thwarted Ed's attempt to murder a stand-in for Melanie, everybody was beyond tired.

EPILOGUE

To: Bbarrett@circle.com
From: Rbarrett@uwash.edu
Re: Wedding bells etc.
Date: 11/26/01 10:19:44

Mom,

Sol really got our attention when he tapped his knife on his wineglass and announced that you two are going to get married! Mark and I had just about gotten used to your living in sin too. Mark thinks you two should have a big love-in-type picnic wedding with sixties music on Pier A in Hoboken. But I think it should be more elegant, maybe on one of those dinner cruises around the tip of Manhattan. Or would that be too sad now? Grandma Sadie has a bet with Sofia that you'll elope. We all think it's pretty cool that Sol seems almost like his old self again.

Speaking of cool, Aveda fits in really well with our family. She didn't seem to notice when Mark and I were screaming at each other about whether to baste the turkey with white wine and butter like Martha says or to use Kitchen Bouquet like we always did. I'm glad she's seen him at his lamest and doesn't mind. And Aveda got really into it when Grandma Sadie started a pool to bet on your wedding date or where you two would go for your honeymoon. (Isn't it awesome how fast Grandma Sadie's ankle has healed? I wanted to give her some physical therapy for it, but she said she didn't need it. That's totally amazing for someone her age. Go, Grandma!) And speaking of Grandma Sadie, it was so funny how she couldn't stop talking about visiting the Bada Bing Club. She was totally psyched about that tour of Soprano sites she and Sofia took.

Gotta go, but thanks for the pics of the new kitchen. Keith and I downloaded them and drooled. It's like a kitchen in a magazine. Thank goodness Charlie and Ilona found someone to finish it so fast. It's so weird that Ed would turn psycho. Who knew? My mom, that's who! Way to go, Mom.

Love,
Rebecca

ABOUT THE AUTHOR

Jane Isenberg taught English to urban community college students for close to thirty years. She has been writing mysteries ever since she experienced her first hot flash. Her copies of *Modern Maturity* are delivered to her home in Issaquah, Washington, which she shares with her husband Phil Tompkins. Visit her website at *www.JaneIsenberg.com*.

The employees of Thorndike Press hope you have enjoyed this Large Print book. All our Thorndike and Wheeler Large Print titles are designed for easy reading, and all our books are made to last. Other Thorndike Press Large Print books are available at your library, through selected bookstores, or directly from us.

For information about titles, please call:

(800) 223-1244

or visit our Web site at:

www.gale.com/thorndike
www.gale.com/wheeler

To share your comments, please write:

Publisher
Thorndike Press
295 Kennedy Memorial Drive
Waterville, ME   04901